# GET ANOT

Kaz Cooke is an Australian cartoonist,
author and broadcaster.

To Manon.
Just to let you
know how serious
we are

Mary

By the same author
*The Modern Girl's Guide to Safe Sex*
*Keep Yourself Nice*
*The Crocodile Club*
*Real Gorgeous: The Truth About Body and Beauty*
*The Little Book of Stress*
*Get a Grip*
*Lola Montez, The Arts of Beauty* (illus.)
*Women's Trouble* with Ruth Trickey
*The Little Book of Crap* with Simon Weaselpantz

# GET
# ANOTHER
# GRIP

## Kaz Cooke

TEXT PUBLISHING
MELBOURNE AUSTRALIA

## Acknowledgments

Many of these pieces were originally published as columns in the *Australian* newspaper's weekend magazine. Some others were run as articles on the *Australian's* opinion page. A few appeared in the *Sydney Morning Herald*. One was a story for *New Woman* magazine. Bits were part of raves on the Martin–Molloy radio show and wee portions were performed on Melbourne's FOX-FM radio breakfast show at some ungodly hour I can't even *think* about now. Thanks to Steve Fosberry, Candy Baker, Jill Rowbotham, *New Woman* magazine, Tony Martin, Mick Molloy, Sancia Robinson, Peter Grace, Melanie Murphy and Brett McLeod.

The Text Publishing Company
171 La Trobe Street
Melbourne Victoria 3000
Australia

First published 1998

Printed and bound by Griffin Press
on Australian-made Regent 100% recycled offset paper
Designed by Kaz Cooke and Redback Graphix
Typeset in 11.8/15.5pt Bembo by Midland Typesetters

National Library of Australia
Cataloguing-in-Publication data:

Cooke, Kaz 1962 –
Get another grip

ISBN 1 875847 66 9

1. Australian wit and humor. 2. Australia – Anecdotes I. Title.

152.4300994

# CONTENTS

## 4 Fashion & Phoofing

## 5 Haughty Culture

## 6 Politicklish

## 7 Mag Slags & Underbelly Telly

## 8 Playtime

## 9 Time Orf

To

Aunty Glenda Merle Haystack Jones

# 1
# Raunch, Romance
# & Relationships

# Not Actually Rudey-Nudey

Look around on public transport and see how many women are reading 'women's' erotic novels. Dead give-aways include a flushed dial, a slightly startled expression, a trembling hand clutching a well-thumbed book, and the odd speculative glance around the conveyance.

While not actually rudey-nudey or anything, the covers do convey a sense of the business at, ahem, hand, with a fair bit of lingerie, the odd cleavage heaving from a pirate shirt or a spot of hooded glowering in the peepers depart-ment. And none o' your Fabio types either—it's all girlies on the cover written by girlies for girlies. Adult girlies.

It's a real conversation stopper once a fellow pas-senger has clocked the cover. 'Hello miss...oh. Ah. Hoo. Stewardess—a large whiskey and twelve Prozacs, please.'

Erotica is now big business—Australians Linda Jaivin and Tobsha Learner have racked up big sales with their stories of varied scenarios involving fruit or dentist chairs. In the English erotic novels people just keep whacking each other. Girlies galore with smarting buttockulor regions being submissive to Mills and Boon-type chaps with whips and for whom no means yes, yes, oh baby, yes.

So the sudden marketing push of the English Black Lace series of erotic novels is a surprise. The press release claims that 'Black Lace will not publish a novel that... suggests that women should be, or enjoy being, subjugated to men, or which includes rape, bloodshed or wounding or emotional anguish as a result of sexual activities.' No, what usually happens in a spanking novel is that the woman is emotionally anguished by her secret desires to be dominated and whacked against her will and *then* finds happiness when she gives in.

The Black Lace book *Handmaidens of Palmyra*, for instance, has more bondage than a rope factory and a lot of non-consenting sex. Cruel Prince Alif (you know the type) tells Samoya that she must be lashed. 'No!' she cries, 'twisted on her chains', and then other stuff happens to her which, described here, would ensure twenty-seven complaint letters from rural Queensland.

Kerri Sharp, a senior editor of the books at (hello) Virgin Publishing, describing herself as a pro-sex feminist, is used to defending the trend. 'Many female fantasies are about imagining oneself in sexual situations where one's dominance or submissiveness is a factor...most people tend to want to surrender responsibility. They don't want to be ashamed by having to ask for what they really want.' (Especially if it's actually a cup of tea.)

'Spanking—and other games of dominance and submission—is about "naughty fun" and not about women being subjugated to men economically or socially. Spanking and SM games are more like cowboys and Indians for adults.' (Although, as I recall, nobody ever wanted to be the Indians.)

Ms Sharp says surveyed readers want a spanking (so to speak). 'Many of the respondents who have submissive or spanking fantasies are highly educated professional women with above-average incomes.' Makes you wonder whether women with no money or power and real violent partners

4

fantasise about pushing them under a big, sexy bus.

Luckily, the new Black Lace releases include *Desire under Capricorn*, set in Australia in the 1870s, a jolly sexy time if you don't count diphtheria, syphilis and endless camping. This one has some rather promising lines such as 'Butch shed his trousers as swiftly as his mate had done. Emily looked in wide-eyed wonder.' (Perhaps she was a novelty boxer-shorts buyer for the first Grace Brothers department store.)

A quick flip of the book revealed no spanking and our heroine, between bodices, declaring, 'I will neither be treated with disrespect nor tolerate being roughly handled.' Let's hope Supreme Court judges take more notice of *Desire under Capricorn* and real life than *Handmaidens of Palmyra* when deciding whether no means no.

Anyway, I'm just off to have a quick squizz at *Nadya's Quest* in which she is 'trembling from the wicked caresses of the young sailor'. Shut up. I'm *researching*.

This week's ideas come from an unknown philanthropist called Lenny, who approached me at a public event and thrust out some photocopied pages. For yea, Lenny had found in a library a tome called *Once a Week Is Ample or the Moderately Sensual Victorian's Guide to the Restraint of Passions*. Phwooooaarrrr, eh? Good on you, Lenny.

The book is by Gerard MacDonald who has collected the advice of 'experts' to nineteenth-century chaps about such matters as their superiority to women and the insatiable carnal desires of girlies. I agree entirely with our prime minister who told pesky women's groups that he's not ashamed of being a 'traditionalist'. I think it's time we reissued the following, from MacDonald's book, as government policy.

A young man wondered what would happen to a girl if he were to 'tempt her, as yet unfallen, to stray from the Highway of Virtue'. He would be the cause of her ending in a hospital ward, 'where the betrayed and outcast woman, one mass of physical corruption, loathsome alike to the smell and the sight, and hardly recognisable as a human being, dies, and without ceremony, is hurried, in a (cheap) coffin to a pauper's grave.'

In other words, the filthy moll trod the Lane of Hyperbole and ended up down the Cul de Sac of Righteous Christian Nastiness without private health insurance. So, what the hell, go for it: there's no consequences for the bloke. Because each and every wanton jezebel is a pension-grabbing temptress descended from Eve, that shameless, fruit-fondling old fanny-waggler. (Oh, stuff the sexual discrimination commissioner.)

'Girls who are natural and would like to be well-married would do well to avoid education, remembering that the personal advantage to the highly educated woman impairs her usefulness as a mother. Those who overtax their vital energies by an intellectual strain...ought to accept a voluntary celibacy.' (What does he *mean*, voluntary?) Furthermore, low-cut dresses cause consumption in men and a woman wants to feel 'ruled'.

What is the 'Effect of the Sexual Relation'? 'Sometimes those who previously seemed hearty and strong lose their bloom and vigour and become emaciated and miserable. Sometimes not.' (Sometimes women will go gallivanting about with a dirty great grin on their face but we are forming a Senate committee led by someone whose name starts with H to oversee the stamping out of this lascivious and unseemly—what's the word?—satisfaction.)

Men, your wives ought to wear loose clothing 'unless you actively desire a family of alcoholic idiots'. And you chaps should get a grip on yourselves, but not too rhythmically. If you are troubled by 'night-time emissions', a Dr Acton recommends a bedtime enema with a pint of ice-cold water. Which could be quite bracing.

A truly inspired Mr Ethelmer explained that the 'menstrual habit' was not 'an indispensible requisite of either health or maternity' and in fact the 'obnoxious phenomenon' was caused by the earlier behaviour of 'savages', and would soon die out.

Obviously.

# CHECK OUT THE CHIKOS

Another fabulous tale from advertising—a proposal to squirt lemon-scented vodka fragrance at people from bus-stop ads. Quite a lot of squirting goes on from the bus stops near our place but you'd have to cut out the middle man, or 'middle derro' to blame the alcohol or advertising industries.

If an ad gives you the irrits you can no longer complain to the Advertising Standards Council. It has ridden into a big colour-adjusted sunset, picking a path through film crews, smooth-cornering four-door family wagons, Marlboro men and teenage boys drinking PEPSI MAX! and bending sii-iiideways into camera lenses.

We have been alerted to the council's deadness by the Catholic Church and the Women's Electoral Lobby who wanted to complain about the film poster for *The People Versus Larry Flynt*. This movie canonises a free-speech activist whose magazine ran depictions of women in degrading sexual situations up to, and including, rape.

(Mr Flynt happily went on doing this for many years until he foolishly offended a *man* depicted in a degrading sexual situation, who was advised by a lawyer he might win a case against Mr Flynt, and the ensuing events are the stuff of the movie.)

It looks like the film poster has been designed to offend women who don't like parts of women's bodies being used for titillating selling points, to offend people who think it's blasphemy to portray a crucified porn king, and

8

to offend people who believe the US flag should not be wrapped around Woody Harrelson's willy.

Personally, I think everyone has a point—you should be allowed to show and say things (and here I draw the line at violent pornography, child pornography, newspaper classified ads on Valentine's Day referring to Snookums and Cuddlebottom, and pictures of Peter Costello's smile) without fear of being censored or jumped all over by a cashed-up bunch of politicians who won't reform the libel laws.

Equally, and perhaps even more importantly, people are also allowed to complain if it gives them the irrits for any reason, for example an unavoidable arse-filled billboard advertising shampoo or an enormous street poster of Elle McFeast with a centrefold expression and the word 'BREASTS' writ huge below.

Or take (please) the latest campaign for Chiko Rolls, stumbled over in research about the history of surfie chicks. (In the tradition of Jewish jokes told by Jews and poof comments made by gay folk, girls may call themselves chicks but boys ought not, to be on the safe side.)

'Chiko Rolls are the most eaten and asked for take-away food by males aged between 18 and 25', says the ad agency. Presumably in a bold bid to attract women, the agency has come up with a brilliant plan of a poster showing a young man looking out to sea while Katrina Long, *Inside Sport's* 1995 model of the year and now known as (here's a career boost) Niki the Chiko chick, sits on the back of a Harley looking bored and clutching a cold Chiko Roll (as you do).

To accompany the poster is a radio ad, sung by a bloke who tries to be George Thorogood ('Bad to the Bone'), but who succeeds only in being bad to the epidermis:

> Let me tell you 'bout this chicky by the name of Nicky
> Whose been asking for it for a while.
> She said, 'Are you gonna give me what I'm thinkin?'
> I said, 'Nicky tonight's the night.'
> It'd be a bit of fun if I could finally give her one
> But I had to use a bit of self control
> 'Cos I gotta tell you it's a long way to the shop
> When you want to give a chick a roll.
> That's the night my Nicky got into a Chiko
> 'Cos I finally gave her one
> Get into a Chik
> Get into a Chik
> Get into a Chiko Roll.

No need to call for the return of the Advertising Standards Council. If he thinks that little effort is going to convince a woman to let him 'give her a roll', he'll be celibate until he's at least fifty-six.

# A GLUT OF BACHELORS

You'll be relieved to hear that *Cleo* magazine has chosen the Bachelor of the Year from a robust field of pectoral flaunters: swimmer, Scott Miller. Mr Miller is keen on the sort of woman who 'has a career and isn't clingy or possessive'.

My giddy aunt, what a relief. Nobody wants a Bachelor of the Year whose ideal woman languishes around the house all day in shorty pyjamas and high-heeled mules planning her next stalking foray.

Bachelor, as a concept, seems to have maintained a rather thrilling cachet of man-about-town-boysiness, although for many years 'confirmed bachelor' was reporters' code for He Came from the Planet of Pooves.

(This usually manifested itself as a photo caption under a picture of a bloke wearing a cravat laughing uproariously at the extemporised cleavage of a heaving socialite brandishing a Pimms shandy. The caption would say: 'Confirmed bachelor Monty "Dorothy" Dix enjoys a joke with Citronella Aulderbag (Mrs) at the opening of Ben Hur on Ice. Citronella is wearing a flapping Dior.')

Spinster, on the other hand, conjures up an elderly frail in a serviceable twin-set who buys one chop for dinner and gives her chum Marjorie a lift to lawn bowls in a Hillman Minx with original upholstery.

So what can we expect from a modern bachelor? Perhaps a man who can knock up a carport out of an old cereal box, a Phillips-head screwdriver and some Tarzan's

Grip (Mr Handy). Or maybe somebody who knows a merkin crab lure from a galvanised crampon (Mr Outdoor). A man who can whip up a quail spleen risotto (Mr Indoor) or a guy who is bonking the entire rhythm section of the Married Ladies Senior Precision Marching Contingent (Mr Backdoor).

There are many other bachelor options, including Mr Tragic Artiste (puppy-dog eyes, infuriatingly boyish fringe, takes twelve years to write frightful novel), Mr Social Challenge (beard, socks, sandals, photographic memory for weather statistics), and Mr Hoon (low-slung trouser arrangement, doughnuts—fat-fried or in unpaved carpark).

You may have already encountered Mr Right, Mr Approximate and Mr Run for the Hills. (Mr Pretendy Bachelor can be identified by a mysterious tan-line on his ring finger, a bassinette in the back seat or a political career in tatters.)

Prospective bachelors seeking a role model should steer well clear of Cool Shavin' Ken, a Barbie Doll accessory on display in any comprehensive toy shop. Cool Shavin' Ken comes with a teensy bottle of imaginary Old Spice aftershave and what looks suspiciously like a merkin crab lure on his noggin. If forced to an opinion, I'd have to say that Cool Shavin' Ken looks as if he's had some kind of psychotic episode while eating a Vegemite sandwich. You couldn't take him anywhere.

*Cleo*'s editor, Gina Johnson, says that Scott Miller 'embodies the essence of the quintessential Australian bachelor'. Could it be, however, that Gina's stud-spotters did not canvass the entire range of Aussie bachelors, as merely touched on here?

There's an enormous GLUT of bachelors in Australia, from Mr Terrific Dunderhead to Mr Blindingly Intellectual. Everywhere you hear women complaining that they are spoiled for choice and tired of being squired around by brilliantly interesting men. *Cleo* could have expanded their list to five million eligible bachelors, no worries.

How could they have overlooked the president of the Campbelltown Young Liberals, Mr John Justice? Mr Justice, a 140-kilo heavyweight boxer, this week told *Herald Sun* journalist Jeff Wells a thing or two about life, quoting a philosopher called Mr Nietzsche: 'Man should be trained for war, women for the recreation of the warrior. All else is folly.' (Mr Nietzsche would have been a thrilling dinner companion, obviously.)

Those girlish hearts among you who thrill to this very notion may start brushing up quick smart on your warrior-entertaining skills. Mr Justice can be located at his father's pub where he is providing, ahem, security services, and insisting that Paul Keating is a communist. Don't forget your Scrabble set.

Pregnancy makes a lot of people forget their manners. They go right up to a stranger and put their hands all over her belly. They say to acquaintances: 'Are you trying to get pregnant? Don't you want to have children? Are you pregnant yet?'

As an etiquette adviser I must say pregnant women are a look-don't-touch proposition, no matter how tempting you find it to just bound up and start fondling them. Besides, your tiny hands are germy, and she can ill-afford exploding sinuses right at the moment, thank you.

And as for blithe interrogators, a swag of comments will have to do, including: 'I forgot', 'It's the poo which makes the proposition untenable, I'm afraid', 'You'll be the first to know' and the surprisingly effective, 'Why do you want to know?'

My paramour, the coiff-king Des Tiny, recently bought a small minivan to transport his throbbingly expanding business, Mistress Beverley's Mobile Wiglets and Toupees to the Stars: Discretion a Must, a touring cornucopia of fancy-tressed wig-stands and unassuming fluffy parts for the noggin. This vehicular purchase, along with moving to a larger turret to accommodate Mistress Beverley Inc and my own ambitions in the direction of platform-thong decorating, led to much unseemly speculation.

Combine real estate move, larger motor car and any hint of an enigmatic smile which one cultivates to cover a whirling sense of nothing to speak of going on in the brainish region and there is an immediate up-the-duffian calculation on the part of bystanders.

It would be an enormous advantage to have a couple of loinfruit called Damone and Angelicabelle who say the most divinely hilarious things or make one ponder the meaning of modern art but, frankly, they haven't turned up.

I practised, just in case, on a Tamagotchi baby, one of those tiny digital games the real kids are whingeing for. Des and me turned the game on, called our electronic screen-baby Fred and pressed Start. There was a button to be pressed when Fred produced what the instructions called 'dung'. And buttons to see Fred's weight and age; to play paper, scissors, rock with him; give him rice or a bottle; or 'discipline' him. (Unfortunately there was no Child Protection Unit button.)

Des would bound in from a day of demanding clients saying things like 'I want the Joan Sutherland', 'Just a little on the top, thanks', 'I want a natural, Marie Antoinette ringlet look' and 'For Christ's sake don't make me look like Ted Drane' and Des, breathless and tender, would ask, 'How's Fred?'

And at night, flushed with the bloom of mothering a newborn, I would report, 'Try the cutlery drawer', 'Haven't seen him all day' or 'I left him in a cafe'. Or more often, the simply poignant diagnosis, 'Well, Fred's dead.' Bloody depressing game if you ask me.

No, it has to be said: motherhood is the hardest and most honourable job in the world. And let's face it, I'm not likely to get a reference from Fred.

# WIFE LIFE

Polygamy is on the rise among your more fundamentalist Mormons in the Mormon-dominated state of Utah in the USA: the *Sunday Times* of London reports that 35,000 people live in polygamous households.

Polygamy is not for women, you understand. Oh no, indeed, women having several toyboys around would be, well, unseemly, obviously and...ooh...sorry. Where was I?

Anyway, these fringey Mormon men have a direct line from a bloke called God, or a source very close to Him, which says that women are not equal but different, and quite useful items around the house, so the more the better.

It is amazing what God will tell you to do if you put your mind to it. Let us—please—not forget the startling efforts of Joseph Jeffers who legged it from the Baptists in 1943, announced he was Christ, and therefore needed to take a much younger woman into the desert to impregnate her. He went to Florida, presumably to learn more about geography and his own divinity.

Similarly, the fringey Mormon men tend to take younger and younger wives as time goes on. What an intensely *spiritual* idea. A thirty-eight-year-old chiropractor in a polygamous turkey-farming valley (good grief) had a thirty-seven-year-old wife and three children before he decided to marry a twenty-one-year-old.

The chiropractor sternly explained, 'There's no three-in-a-bed stuff in this house.' No, he's a chiropractor and knows the consequences. And besides, that would be, like, weird. 'Our sexual relationships are a sacred thing.' Uh-huh.

The *Sunday Times* also reported on several other 'families' including one bloke with ten wives and twenty-eight children. He must be a terrific dad to each and every one of the twenty-eight little individuals, don't you reckon? There's probably a great party trick where he can remember most of their names.

One suspects the joke, in some small ways, might be on the men. The women are reportedly often good friends who, rather than fight jealously over the chance to go to sleepy-byes with the man of the house, are more likely to roll their eyes: 'My turn again, dammit. Stir the custard till I get back, would you?'

The official Mormon church, meanwhile, calls these baby-making factory-line, polygamous families 'whore-doms'. Yes, traditionally, religions are tremendously generous to women. That's right, there's your choice of Mormon womanhood: whore or saintly vessel of smaller fundamentalist Mormons.

And while pompous self-appointed experts in Australia are lining up to say single mothers should have their second and subsequent children taken away from them because they're a drain on the state (I saw a toady man saying this on 'A Current Affair' recently, serves me right for channel-hopping), the blokes are hardly mentioned.

What of the men who merrily shoot sperm and then shoot through? What of the contraception companies, who have yet to come up foolproof? What of blokes who have twelve children to three different women and can't support them, fringey-Mormon or otherwise? How come the women are the ones who get the nasty labels and the disapproval?

'Ultimately,' the polygamous chiropractor says, of choosing a new wife, 'It is the man's choice.' No kidding.

# THE RUBBER FASCINATORS WITH THE OOMPH PANELLING

We at Women Who Want To Be Obscenely Wealthy (WWWOW)—if you'd like to join, please send membership fee of $3.2 million to me immediatement, also any big tiaras, pearls the size of plover's eggs, ermine-trimmed frippery, etc—yes, we at WWWOW were poised to publish our steamy sex and shopping novella, *Men Are from Mars, Women Are from Albury* when this John Gray, PhD pipped us at the post and sold twelve gerzillion copies of *Men Are from Mars, Women Are from Venus*.

Well, we later tried to flog *Men Are from Mars, Let's Get Over There*; we had a fizzer of a bidding war over the manuscript of *Well, Can We Go Back to Venus Now?*, and failed to excite any interest in *If Men Are from Mars, What Happened at Immigration?* Although Janine did do quite well with her suddenly rare story, 'I Didn't Marry an Alien'.

Dr John cleaned up when he realised that due to an oversight at the plant, men and women come without operating instructions, and if he invented a manual people everywhere would fall upon him with gladdened cries and slavishly build entire lives around page 27.

And now the Doc has whirled through again with his new book and lecture tour, *Mars and Venus in Love: Inspiring and Heartfelt Stories of Relationships That Work*. He and his wife Bonnie are on the back cover in what must be a picture used in an ad for their dentist some years ago, when they needed the cash. (It's way time for a book called *Sure Americans Are from Mars, But Where on Earth Do Their Teeth Come from?*)

I didn't read *Men Are from Mars, Women Are from Venus* because I was washing my hair at the time. And also, the man of my dozings, the robust yet windswept Mr Des Tiny OBE, comes from Dubbo so I didn't think I'd need it. But lately Mr Tiny has been seen in the company of the sort of woman who markets exotic knits, the dreaded Shazza di Boomdeeyay, an Aran-hearted cable-knit fondler if ever I saw one and, although he says they only discuss raglan sleeves through the ages and the rules of whist, I plunged in to the latest manual.

Tom wrote, 'If I've been in the cave for a few days, when I'm back, I do something special, like bring her flowers or clean up the kitchen.' (Top points for getting 'special' and 'clean up the kitchen' in one sentence.) Others write praising the Doc's intructions to leave a husband in his metaphorical cave without insisting he behave like a socialised human being. (In the old days this was called, 'Ignore him, dear, he's probably sulking.')

Men wrote to the Doc to say they finally learned to listen, even if they had to pretend to be interested, because the women needed to talk. (This used to be called 'Best to let her bang on about it, mate, she'll get it out of her system eventually.') Marsha reported that she now says to her Roger, 'I need to be real Venusian right now, you don't have to say anything.' Lordy. Another wrote, 'Men were not afraid of intimacy, nor did they need years of therapy— they were from Mars.' (Take heed fellas, it's a fab excuse:

'Sorry. Can't communicate. Alien. Going pub.')

So anyway, when my Des got home from a jam-fancy evening with Shazza, I told him he could stay in his cave as long as he liked and I was about to come over a bit Venussy. And you know, the Doc may have something. Because when I put on the French maid's uniform, and the rubber fascinators with the oomph panelling and the antennas, and boldly went where I hadn't been before, things did seem to start looking up.

# VIVE LA DIFFERENCE, YOU BITCH

Men are generally considered more likely to be able to think about only one thing at a time. Women are more likely to cry. Men are more likely to be unable to tell the difference between a skirt and a dress. Women are more likely to be nurturing. Men don't clean up the kitchen. Bollocks. Sorry, ovaries.

There are really three main differences. One: The topographical dangly bits. Two: Men are more likely to eat boxed breakfast cereal. Three: If a man and a woman miss a relationship/job offer/catch the woman is more likely to say 'I'm hopeless and it's all my fault' and a man is more likely to say 'The sun was in my eyes, my Y-fronts were on backwards and the ball moved the wrong way'. Frankly, we can learn a lot from the male version.

In toy shops the boys' section is full of cars, weapons, and Action-Man dolls. Coming soon: Emotionally Crippled Trevor with Detachable Semi-Automatic Weapon. The girls' section is awash with every conceivable variation on hot-pink, full of dolly dress-ups and wee tea sets. This does not stop girls from going vroom vroom. ('And get away from that teapot Jason, what are you, a poofter?')

In the newsagent, the alleged women's magazine section contains coverlines such as 'Girl Crushes—Can a Friendship Go Too Far?' (Dear editor: Not if you're a lesbian); 'Our Baby Weighed Less than a Tomato' and 'Paint a Chair' (on the same cover); 'Dieting For Jesus—How God Made Me Slim'; and in the young women's section

*Dolly* offers 'Fun Ways to Burn Fat Fast (Bust That Butt)'. One hopes growing girls get time-out for a breather between Barbie and Butt-Busting.

The so-called men's magazine section offers *Awesome Holdens*; *British Esquire* (Quiz: How Handy Are You?); and *Scale Aircraft Modelling* featuring plans for a Luftwaffe Tank Buster. (Uh, guys, the war's over.) *Sports Illustrated* and *Sports Monthly* both feature large cover photographs of the well-known sport of cleavage rigging. (*Amazing Bosoms Monthly* and *Really Enormous Buttocks Ahoy* magazines were obscured by short men in beige bodyshirts who wouldn't make eye contact.)

*English for Him* magazine sent some reporters to 'swap lives'—the male reporter had to buy tampons, have a bikini wax, wear high heels, run with pretend bosoms and swallow one of his own bodily fluids (this is all true).

The female reporter had to wee standing up, buy a porno magazine, eat a red-hot curry, fart, change a car wheel and wear the same undies for three days (I'm hoping this must be an English thing rather than a bloke thing.)

Just as all this research was becoming a tad hornswoggling, an alternative presented itself: *Dog Showbiz:The Annual 96–97*. Surely this litany of animal splendidness would show us up for the gender-obsessed we are.

Actually the entries for show dogs read more like a refreshingly candid lonely-hearts column. 'Miss Sarah Hemstock (UK) Mahogany brindle. Outstanding bitch in superbly fit condition but not over mature for her age. Beautiful movement, moved freely and with drive from well-flexing hindquarters. A pleasure to go over.'

Jeez, get her phone number.

If only people were described with such clarity. The dogs are variously described as 'standing at stud to approved bitches, a proven sire, outgoing personality, a poser, wormed, having dark round eyes with plenty of space between [this is something we all look for, space between the eyes], a mover, with tail, a showman, with current clear eye certificate'. Even a Bichon Frise which looks like an accident at the fluff factory is lauded as a champion goer.

It all goes to show that whatever the stereotypical differences, everyone is a deeply gorgeous individual with their own pulsatingly fascinating qualities, and we're all just utterly lovable examples of explodingly admirable humanity underneath. Unless you're an outstanding bitch or a poser with worms.

# 2
# Progress: Science, Inflatable Insect Willies & So On

# The New Cold and the Squoozy Woozy Leg Virus

You may have noticed some of the new viruses that are about, increasingly ubiquitous, ineluctable and opprobrious—with scientific names that are even harder to spell than that. We hear tell of viruses which merely snicker in the face of antibiotics and pull rude faces at echinacea.

Here we present the year's wrap-up of Nouveau Lurgies we have come to know and loathe, a matter we have spent the entire bloody year rehearsing.

## The New Tummy Upset Virus
In this condition, your stomach is not so much upset as discombobulated and hysterical. Your tummy is turned upside down, you are drenched in sweat and your head hurts. (If these symptoms are accompanied by wanting emphatically to kiss somebody, you're in lust.)

## The New Cold
Remarkably like the old cold in almost every respect, except it can be accompanied by symptoms of nearly anything else at the same time. The New Cold rarely travels alone these days. Its companions can include an attractive chest rash with hot pink blotches, rapid eye movement, a goatee beard or the sudden facility to speak in tongues.

The New Cold is a lucky dip in which only a few things remain constant: head full of clag, severe and noticeable stupidity, the shedding of skin layers in or about the nostrils, wheezing, sneezing, whingeing, snurrfling, snonking, scuffling, snoring and whistling through bits you didn't know were there.

## THE SUMMER COLD
Not to be confused with Summer Pudding, a divinely scented and delightful sugary concoction of white bread and seasonal berries of rich hues such as strawberries, blackberries and blueberries, the Summer Cold is when the sun is shining, the world is skipping about and you're standing there wondering what happens if you don't wash for three days, dressed in waffle-weave long johns, Explorer socks and an old wheat bag and yelling at visitors from the verandah: 'Don't come any closer! I'm a Snot-Gurgling Troll!'

Advantage: Can tell the story of 'Billy Goats Gruff' to small children on the phone in quite a realistic manner.

## THE NEW FLU
The New Cold but with more sweating and maybe your chest and throat explode. The New Flu is no longer called 'The Russian' 'The Chinese' or 'The African' as they ran out of continents. It is now called 'a nasty virus'. Doctors' instructions: 'Nothing we can do. Out of our hands. Too spooky. Probably from outer space. Go to bed for four years and wait.'

## THE SQUOOZY WOOZY LEG VIRUS
Accompanies any of the above and is generally characterised by a distinct feeling of Presleyitis about the knees. Patients find that while their legs are collapsing to jelly for

no particular reason a nanosecond of amusement can be obtained by grabbing a ukelele and shouting, 'And it's a-one for the money, two for the…bugger it, how does that go again?' before collapsing onto a divan for the duration.

## THE NEW FEELING A BIT OUT OF SORTS
An overwhelming sense of morbid fear and moral dread, seizing the afflicted with a terrible sense of doom. It's all right, it's only the government. At least you've got your health.

# WIGGED-OUT BUGS

Will these fabulous inventions never stop? Cloning is old news now that people in England can buy chocolate-flavoured vegetables—so the kiddies will get into them. Vegans will soon be offered turnip-flavoured chocolate. And Australia's place as the clever country has been assured as we now lead the world in devices to inflate insect genitals.

Whoopsie, and I beg your pardon, vicar? Somebody call Barbara Windsor, it is 'Carry on up the CSIRO' time, with *New Scientist* reporting that an Australian engineer has invented a small (natch) gizmo for inflating the weeny weenies of dead insects, all the better to measure them with because size, in the racy world of entomology, is still important.

Marcus Matthews, an insect checker-outerer with the CSIRO, says the new device, called a Phallobuster (and not to be confused with the Ironman/supermodel style stomach-crunching arrangements advertised on morning telly) should catch on—at $4200 it's the perfect gift for somebody who has everything. But there's a warning attached. Mr Matthews says when it comes to inflating a moth's waggly part, 'Unless you are very careful, it is easy to smash the specimen to bits.' I know the feeling.

I think it's important that somebody puts the CSIRO entomology willy-puffers in touch with a performance artiste in San Francisco who is using live bee-buzzing on stage to accompany her musical offerings.

*Ambience* magazine reports that Miya Masaoka plucks at her koto ('a zither-like instrument'), bangs on it or drags her bow across its strings, creating sounds 'that might give way in an instant to screeching, abrasive noise'. Meanwhile, a hive of 3000 bees goes berserk in a tank on stage. Miya explains, 'The bee gig started when I had this vision of me on stage with all kinds of unwanted things in cages—flies, mice, rats, creepy crawly things, and they would be amplified. But the rats caused problems with the health code.' Damned critics. This followed Miya's very successful performance-art piece where she lay naked on a table and, while hissing 'Madagascar', cockroaches crawled on her and her assistant played Indian bells. Get down.

In the meantime, fabulous advice continues to pour forth from our local magazine sector. *Cleo* advised recently on how to seduce a man. Tips include: 'Catch him off guard.' Yeah, wait until he's asleep and then leap at him from the wardrobe screaming, 'I must have you!' Scrape him off the ceiling and go at him.

Also, it is recommended that you pinch him. Then he'll pinch you. And then you'll be rolling on the ground together. Well, either that or he'll think you're a fruitcake and walk quickly away to the airport and catch the next flight to a place where there are grown-ups.

The best *Cleo* seduction hint though, is 'act kittenish'. If you don't get your dinner on time, whine endlessly in a high-pitched voice. And then wee on the carpet. What bloke could resist?

# PARTY POOPERS

What's the difference between a scientist and a party pooper? Not a lot, as two new reports inform us that breathing is bad for you and if you're half-starved you'll live longer. Oh, fab.

According to a *Sunday Telegraph* report from London, the home of hairshirtery, black pudding and government ministers who have sex with citrus fruit, comes the news that oxygen accumulates in our body, damaging cells until we become the victims of 'oxidative stress'. Eventually, as the *Telegraph* puts it, 'We grow old and die.' (Unless we're bored to death first by scientists.)

The discovery that we're going to grow old and die is a bit like setting up a think-tank which reports, 'If you lie in the middle of the road you're likely to get run over' or 'If you go around wearing a small dachshund on your head people will start to think you might be a trifle deranged'.

The other mob of scientists we take as our control group today have announced test results showing that normal mice eat 100 calories a week and live until they're three, but mice fed fifty calories a week will live 40 per cent longer. (That's 40 per cent more time to be a hungry, grumpy, bored research mouse.) The researchers are excited by similar results in half-starved worms and fish.

Is it significant, do you think, that one of the mice researchers is from the Southern Methodist University in Dallas? Is this the thin edge of the 'No fun is good for you' school of theology, medicine and purse-lipped interfering old creepism? Are they working on a secret 'Dancing makes you go blind' project? Funds must be released immediately for the purpose of half-starving a whole lot of scientists to see how much they like it.

Of course, if the scientists are right there are very disquieting repercussions. Old folks' homes will be filled with ex-supermodels, with verandahfuls of old models saying things like, 'Hey Elle, are those my false teeth you're wearing?' and 'No lunch for me thanks, Cyndi, I had half a sardine last September'. 'I'm 109 and I haven't had any fun for forty-eight years and by jingo, I'm hungry. If this goes on I'll have to eat my breast implants.'

One of the researchers suggests that to live longer, people over twenty years old can try keeping their weight at 10 to 25 per cent below their 'set weight', which is defined as 'the weight that the body naturally tends towards in the absence of outside influences such as a spate of heavy business lunches'. (Especially in people who don't have business lunches, believed to be 99.99 per cent of the global population.) The researcher warns that to avoid malnutrition the dieting should be conducted 'only under strict medical supervision'. But I think I speak for us all when I say to this researcher: 'Oh, just shut up.' Another way to avoid malnutrition is not to try such a stupid idea in the first place just so you can be miserable for longer before getting old and dying just like the rest of us, whom you will find in the dining room inhaling the custard.

One possible reason for this silly behaviour by scientists is that they have seen the *Elle Decoration* magazine cooking pages. Here, you can learn of the dishes of Celia Lyttleton, who has got hold of a 1932 cookbook and revived the idea of 'futurist cooking'. She elucidates: 'Quantities are a little vague. Imagine you are a four-year-old.' (I fail to see how smearing Vegemite on the dog can be seen as thrilling new cuisine.)

One of her recipes is 'whisk a bowl of cream until it looks like a cloud. Stir in some icing sugar, then serve piled up in a bowl, scattered with grated [lemon] peel and surrounded by a ring of strawberry jam.' (Then throw it in the bin and go out and strangle a scientist. You'll feel so much more *alive*.)

## CREATIVE SCIENCE

There's a court case going on about whether Noah really herded all the animals in the world into the ark. I mean, how would you do that?

What a guy!

How could Noah have rounded up a pair of echidnas in the Middle East?

And there must be at least 67,000 species of ants available.

I've just got one thing to say to Noah: you could have made millions of thong-wearers happy, just by putting up the house-full sign before the bull ants were heaved aboard.

# A MUTTER OF TRUST

Did you hear about the doctor who took out a woman's fallopian tube instead of her appendix? 'Oops' isn't quite enough to cover the situation. It's like hearing, 'The pilot inquired as to the whereabouts of the clutch pedal' or 'Coach wants to know if this is lacrosse or snorkeling'. And didn't anyone else SAY something during the operation? You know, like, 'What are you doing, you idiot?'

The newspaper report about the op incident was on the same page as an ad suggesting, 'Don't just vent your spleen, insure it'. If you can find it.

I see a surgeon from time to time (professionally, thank you very much). One of the reasons to trust this surgeon, even though he has a moustache, is that he eats children's lollies between operations. Quite frankly, if he's got the bottle to be seen waving snakes, gobbling musk sticks and grinning licorice at me as I'm wheeled past freezing my arse off on the stainless steel trolley thingo, he's probably got nothing to hide.

Also, when he's explaining my bits to me he doesn't say stuff like, 'See on this ultrasound scan, that's a relief map of the New Hebrides, with your left bosom on the right-hand side. No, actually I think that's an ear lobe. Tell a lie, I think this is an X-ray of a fractured femur. A lemur femur.' This would occasion alarm on my part.

Once upon a time, lying in a hospital bed waiting for the trolley, I noticed that my wristband and bed label clearly read 'Mr Papadopolous'. On requesting a change, to something more appropriate such as the Countess of Ning-Nong or, let's go crazy, my own name, the nurse rolled her eyes. 'Some people,' she said, 'get really neurotic in here.'

This was my only ever bad experience with a nurse. Generally nurses are down-to-earth angels who should be paid approximately their wage squared and given a monthly trip to the Bahamas. It is their manner that makes you trust them. They seem to know exactly what they are doing i.e.: not mistaking a fallopian tube for spaghetti marinara.

The story caught my eye (or elbow) because, in the process of co-writing a book about girly hormones and periods and what can go wrong with them, we are explaining what our organs really look like. The uterus, for example, is the size and shape of a slightly flattened pear. The ovaries are more the size and shape of a large almond or slightly small, flatter googie eggs. The inside diameter of a fallopian tube is so fine it's the size of a piece of sewing cotton. (This is one of the, oh, 486 things which distinguishes it from the appendix.)

Fallopian tubes, like so many girly bits, are named after a bloke. So is the part of the female body, behind the uterus, known as the Pouch of Douglas (what's wrong with the Clutch Purse of Mavis?). Likewise the Pap test and the Bartholin's glands, which lubricate the downstairs department. Forget the moustache for a minny, would you trust a bloke like that? Imagine the party talk:

'What do you do?'

'I, uh, have women's private parts named after me.' (Cloud of dust.)
PS: We apologise for suggesting that the Pouch of Douglas lies behind the uterus. This is inaccurate: it is, of course, much nearer to the Peter Costello.

# A GLASS OF YOUR BEST
## OSCILLATING, THANKS

It's not that I want to be biased about hippy drippy out-there ferals and their bizarrely dumbo well-meaning new-age meanderings, but faced with the advertised virtues of the Grander Living Water Unit, what's a girl to do but lie down in a room and wait for regular deliveries of quince daiquiris?

Check out the ad in this week's *Living Now*, a giveaway hippy newspaper: 'Tomorrow's Natural Technology Today! Better health for humans and animals; Prevention of corrosion in pipes; [the] taste of a waterfall in your glass; everlasting positive vibrations help restore the rivers and lakes.' What could this be?

It's the 'amazing Living Water Energising Unit. The only known manufactured product capable of duplicating nature's ability to infuse water with life-giving frequencies.' What?

An 'information-based advertising segment' next to the ad explains that the water we drink has been killed by damming rivers and 'shoving it insensitively through pipes'. While this conjures up images of people bludgeoning water to death and shoving it rudely down a pipe shouting 'Garn, git!' we must wade on.

The Unit was invented in the 1970s by Johann Grander, who 'discovered that water is a living being which draws energy from the rocks it encounters as it flows around natural contours, that it has a memory and therefore stores information and that it's a cosmic being containing minerals that have their own planets to which they are magnetically drawn.'

(It's true that water has its own memory. Just the other day I was having a discussion with a glass of tap water about the seventies pop group, the Four Seasons. 'Remember that song called "Late December Back in '63"?' said the glass of water.

'Oh what a lady, what a night?' I recalled.

'Complete crap, wasn't it,' remarked the $H_2O$.)

Yes, but what exactly is the Unit? Well, it 'contains a sealed vial of revitalised water which transmits the different electromagnetic frequencies found oscillating within nature to the ordinary water which passes through it (in the same way that sound is transferred to a blank audio tape).'

The advertorial says that 'Australian legislation prohibits claims regarding the specific effect on human health.' But it then goes on to report that when cows drink Unit water they have fewer teat infections, roses last longer in a vase of it and when rough wine is passed through the Unit it comes out tasting 'like a fine old port'. Blimey Teddy.

You'll be wanting the prices: $986 for a kitchen-tap energiser unit, $1882 for a granny-flat sized joint and $2622 for a three-bedroom home. Then you've got your 'penergiser' a pen-shaped unit to drop into a glass of 'water, juice, wine, milk or any liquid' at $179. (Although in my opinion milk has a shocking memory and some glasses of Milo can't even remember what day it is.)

Anyway, I rang the Grander Living Water Unit people and they said there had been a mistake in the article. Apparently the inventor is Austrian, not Australian. According to the advertorial, the Unit has 'made such an impact on staff at the science department of Monash University, they have begun conducting experiments'. The Unit people reluctantly told me the experiments were being conducted at the Gippsland campus.

A spokeswoman for the Monash School of Applied Sciences there said she'd never heard of the water Unit and 'we are definitely not conducting any research into it'.

A spokeswoman for the Unit distributors later explained in a fax that reporting that the testing was happening was 'an error in judgement', and that they did believe that testing had begun. She was keen to point out that tests were done in November last year 'by science graduates at the Centre for Conservation Technology at the Southern Cross University...these trials validated claims pertaining to the effect of Loving Water on effluent...For example a marked reduction in smell...'

I was going to ring up and find out what Loving Water is, but that's about all the oscillating I can take right now. Make mine a daiquiri.

# LIAR, LIAR, GRANTS ON FIRE

News is just in from a study by an American psychology professor: we tell 200 lies a day. Being a big fan of American psychological studies, we might assume that Professor Gerald Jellison (that's what it says here, good ol' Gerry Jelly) studied tobacco company executives, or rodent-resembling philanderers, or the people who run the CIA.

But no. The *Sunday Telegraph* tells us, in an exhaustive survey of, oh, twenty people, Jellsie seems to have found that the worst offenders are people who have a lot of social contact like doctors' receptionists, politicians, journalists, lawyers, psychologists, sales people and shop assistants. There's your problem. Tell us something we don't know. No wonder they tell an average of one lie every eight minutes.

I ask you, *shop assistants*? 'I wouldn't normally say this, Madam, but that tangerine wool jumpsuit is really most flattering. No, indeed, your buttocks bear very little resemblance to three mad whippets fighting in a knitting bag with every step you take. You look a bit like a young Elizabeth Taylor. Everyone will be wearing them this season. Or not, if you'd like to feel a bit special.'

And politicians? 'I wasn't there at the time, and anyway, there is a strange pixie living in the top drawer of my office desk who claims travel allowances when I'm asleep and he eats all the paperwork in little tiny munches, and everything. Um. Look! Over there!' (Sound of running feet.)

41

And as for journalists: 'I'm sure I filed that column. Have you looked down the back of the couch? It was really quite funny. One of my best. I'm sure I faxed it, although it might have accidentally gone to Uganda. Unless the dog ate it or I was abducted by unseemly aliens who probed right up my...yes, all right, I'll get right onto it. Absolutely. Good God, my fax machine is on fire. I'll get back to you.'

Solicitors? 'Well your bill is calculated on $piR^2$ with a ratio of seven Venn diagrams per phone call times ten squillion, which is pretty much standard. I wrote a very long rude letter to somebody and we find the best way to charge for that kind of service is like a suddenly physically impaired bull, by the paragraph. I think you'll find it's very reasonable.'

Sales people: 'If you rub this on your thighs you will immediately be sexually propositioned by rock stars' or 'Mate, you wouldn't want to drive it away without a sub-woofer and a fluffy steering-wheel cover. That might be dangerous.'

Psychologists: 'Of course you're not barking mad. Lots of adults sleep in layers of margarine and cling wrap, clutching a blow-up John Howard doll which they insist on referring to as "Miss Valerie". I think that's sweet.'

Not to mention doctors' receptionists: 'Doctor is in massively important and complex micro-macro brainy-type surgery all day and cannot be reached except in dire emergencies. No, that doesn't include a heart attack...well you may have seen him in loud plaid plus-fours with a jaunty vinyl cap and a set of golf clubs this morning but he only does that to cheer up the patients. YES, while they're anaesthetised. Now sod off.'

Anyway, the *Telegraph* story also provides hints on how to tell when a politician is lying: nose-rubbing, ear-tugging, cuff-pulling (remind you of anybody?), flattening of voice tones, looking sideways and up (trying to conjure a picture or sound), looking at the hand they write with (trying to control their emotions). Or a politician might be lying if a colleague in the vicinity narrows their eyes during the statement. Surely it's more simple than that? For example, a good place to start might be: a politician is lying when the politician's mouth is open.

That's what I love about these deeply scientific psychological studies. They survey twenty Americans in high-lie professions and then the headline reads: 'We All Lie 200 Times a Day'. You may have the utmost confidence in that statement. It was written by a journalist.

# 3
# This Is the Dawning
# of the Age of…
# Whatever

# FERAL BERYL

As the millennium approacheth upon winged gumboots, the world needs a mix of tribes, as people everywhere realise their common interests and stop snapping at each other like ferrets in a bag.

Politicians living in the smog caused by forest fires begun by devouring logging companies must be starting to wonder about the benefits of clearing land at approximately the same rate as a toddler knocks over a stack of wooden blocks.

Farmers, forced off their land by banks, are starting to get an inkling of what it might be like for Aborigines for whom land is their religion, their purpose, their life, their reason itself. Greenies, now with departments of finance, are putting forward plans for economic alternatives to forestry, thinking about what people put out of work might be able to do.

And in Australia, do industry and the government grasp this new spirit of mutual interest? Well, does John Howard wear a posing pouch? No. Even though the rural mob is fully across the fact that greenhouse gases add to the El Nino effect which gives them their daily drought, the PM thinks it's a triumph to have greenhouse gas emissions in the high to hellish zone.

So the millennium needs a new breed of melded citizen and a fairytale might come true...

Once upon these times, Feral Beryl lives on a farm in Queensland. Beryl is a fifty-six-year-old farmer's wife married to Doug (in other words, Doug's a farmer's husband). Beryl has green dreadlocks, a discreet tattoo on her ankle, a pierced navel, a degree in agricultural pharmacology and the best passionfruit sponge in the district.

Last year she spent four months of the year up a pole in Gooloongook Forest trying to save some trees. (She made 47,975 frozen chops for Doug to heat up while she was away. He chucked the tofu.)

Feral Beryl is in constant touch with El Nino predictors worldwide and has about forty-two years experience in animal husbandry, cleaning, finance, mothering, lobbying, scone-perfecting and about three years in chaining herself to environment ministers.

Her hobbies are shiatsu and crocheting those little doilies with the edges weighed down with beads which you put over the top of your glass to stop flies getting in and drowning in your beverage. Beside Feral Beryl's bed is a copy of the 'State of the Environment Report 1996', *Diana: The Biography*, a republic ballot filled out in the affirmative, and a large battery-operated device.

Her eldest son, A River Trevor, is now running eco-canoeing tours through the silver paths of his boyhood from the nearest major town with his partner, Russell Two-Mile Minchin, a Murri friend who is one of the traditional owners of the country. Feral Beryl often sends along fairy cakes to supplement the bush-tucker section of the tour.

Feral Beryl (formerly National Party) will vote for a politician called Feral Cheryl, who says she'll stand for more taxes to provide affordable schools and hospitals, real employment and protecting the environment. The other pollies will think Feral Cheryl's gone flapdoodly right up until every last Beryl votes for her.

PS: After I wrote this piece I found out there is a doll you can buy called Feral Beryl which comes with a merkin and faux marijuana. A different Feral Beryl entirely, I assure you.

# DON'T ROCK THE DREAMBOAT

Another fabulous dream dictionary has fallen into our hands, this one all the more reliable and scientific because it doesn't have an author. After entitling it *Your Innermost Thoughts Revealed. DREAMS: Hidden Meanings and Secrets* the author was probably too exhausted to type his or her own name.

To save you spending $3.95 on it, you may peruse the following summary of the up-to-the-minute publication *DREAMS*, known as 'cobbling'. (Incidentally, if you dream of hurling a cobblestone through a window you will forget something important—page 79.)

'If a young woman dreams that she is a trapeze performer...she will meet a handsome and agreeable man who will eventually propose marriage.' (It does not explain that the handsome and agreeable man will be wasting his time if he is dilly-dallying with a lesbian trapeze performer.)

Appended to 'riot' is the stern admonishment: 'To dream of being in a riot is a warning against luxurious excesses and sensual indulgence. Beware of being too free with persons of the opposite sex.' (Or to get yourself in the mood, peruse footage of Grace Bros stocktaking sales before retiring.)

Rather more hornswoggling is the explanation of dreaming about a pouffe: 'To dream of putting your feet on an ottoman foretells that young people of different foreign origins will visit you and fall in love.' Quite frankly this is not enough information and an unduly pert and tantalising definition. Will the young people fall in love with each other? Will they fall in love with you? What will they say when they arrive?: 'Hello, pouffe-dreamer. I'm a young person ready to fall in love. Put me up.'

One can only speculate about the possibilities of that parliamentary member for Oxley with no manners, Pauline Hanson, dreaming of pouffes, and what she would do when the young, amorous foreigners turn up at her fish and chip shop. Would she boil them in oil or profit from their potato cakes? Perhaps she dreams of 'half-breeds' ('half-breeds'! How terribly nineties of the publisher, Tophi Books of London, to include such an up-to-date term) in which case she should (wait for it) 'beware of treachery'.

There is no entry for dreaming of Pauline Hanson, but perhaps that's in the nightmare dictionary.

Dreaming of wearing emeralds, as one does practically constantly, 'predicts a life of affluence. You will marry into a wealthy and respected old family...riches and social prestige...inheritance of money and real estate.' (Hurry *up*.)

Many of you, I know, will be puzzled over the meaning of your frequent dreams about clambakes. 'A dream of being present at a clambake predicts good times with your friends, but if you cannot eat a large quantity of food, you will be unhappy.' Unless you're Elvis. Other food dreams include eating chop suey at home ('your chances of advancement are slight'), onion (you're going to the circus) and canned lima beans (business disappointments).

In short, one can only advise you to dream of dachshunds, caper sauce, little girls wearing pinafores, freemasonry, being circumcised (do you think the authors were on drugs?), anchovies, cuspidors (eh?) and the hula hula, preferably all at once.

You may be spared the hideous details but suffice it to report that under no circumstances should you dream of the bray of an ass, a hippopotamus in the zoo, custard, ferrets, football full backs (if you don't believe me it's page 139), blondes, or—it's a sacrifice, but we all have to make an effort—huckleberries.

It is only fair to warn you that if you dream of being an old maid you will marry a fiery black-eyed musician, and I hope there'll be enough to go around. If you dream of griddle cakes you will have an affair 'with the next dark-eyed person you meet'. If you are already in a relationship, you may explain this away to your partner by saying firmly, 'It wasn't my fault. I dreamed of griddle cakes.'

In your dreams.

# ALIENS OF ALL SORTS

The Australian Skeptics call their magazine *The Skeptic*, a brilliant stroke of naming logic akin to the Eatmore Poultry Company of Laverton who are advertising their smoked breast fillets with a photo of a sandwich and a woman's large breasts in a low-cut top. (Mysteriously, advertising for their gourmet rissoles does not involve the depiction of a scrotum. Could there be alien involvement?)

Anyway, in *The Skeptic* a writer called Chris Rutkowski says that space aliens are incompetent, a thesis developed by Ufology Research of Manitoba, which invented the Alien INcompetency Theory (AINT) to explain why accounts of alien abductees are so varied, why aliens crash land, why crop circle messages are indecipherable and why aliens never land on the White House lawn. (But not why aliens, faced with airstrip possibilities the size of a major planet, almost always land in North America.)

Mr Rutkowski's article is reprinted from *The Swamp Gas Journal*, associated with the University of Manitoba in Winnipeg, Canada, and if that doesn't take care of any plagiarism accusations, I'm a monkey's uncle (which was a hilarious epigram first made by Oscar Wilde, Dorothy Parker and Harpo Marx while dining with Herman Melville and Ethelred the Unready ['Big Ethel'] at the Wodonga Hotel round table in 1066). Speaking of which, Ambrose Bierce defined plagiarism as 'To take the thought or style of another writer whom one has never, never read.'

As for this incompetent aliens theory—pish tosh. Aliens

are not incompetent. They are bored, bored, bored. Flouncing around for light years in space and every time they get a date with an earthling it turns out to be somebody called Betsy-Sue Trailatrasher of Lubbock, Texas, or a guy with hair scraped right across his noggin from under his left earhole, who buttons his trousers up at armpit level and thinks that Phar Lap became Lyndon LaRouche (no relation to the well-known drag queen Lynda La Rouch-dee-ay, head of MI7).

Suspiciously, aliens only ever make contact with the more inclement bits of the gern lobby who think there's a United Nations-Jewish-Morris-dancing people-who-put-the-milk-in-the-teacup-before-the-tea-femmo-crypto-pinko-weirdo-porno-National Party-baiting conspiracy led by Hillary Clinton and her loyal assistant Princess Panda to suck the life out of righteous men in hats (wives bring a plate), and that bloke who says he thinks the Holocaust was actually a smudge on the lens of a 1942 Box Brownie, and somebody who chats to the dear departed on a shoe phone. This is the sort of person chosen to receive visits from aliens, and I think we can deduce from this that aliens wish to be entertained by *professional* clowns.

If it takes forty-eight trillion light years to get here from Alpha Zenwhatsit, how many games of 'Spotto' do you think those aliens have endured by now, hurtling through space? 'Hey, Zargon, I spy with my little eye (and I do mean singular) something beginning with...S.'

'Shut up or I'll zork you.'

'Oooh, temper, temper.' The reason why aliens eschew

Burkina Faso or the Opera House for a crash landing in America is because they've heard that's where Disneyland is. No, all right, that's fanciful. Actually, they're trying to get a guest spot on 'The X-Files'.

In the same issue of *The Skeptic*, a Barry Williams writes that the famous 'Alien Autopsy' film which appeared on TV screens around the world late in 1995 is, and I think you ought to sit down, a bit fishy. 'I felt,' he says, 'that there was just an indefinable something wrong with what was shown on the film.'

Barry says it's partly because there were only two pathologists and one camera operator working on the alien's body. 'This is very unlikely in a genuine case of an alien autopsy.' Quite right. In a genuine alien autopsy the pathologists wear party hats. And low-cut tops.

# 13 PLUS 13 IS 26: SPOOKY!

It's Friday the Thirteenth. Not that one believes in any of the pish tosh, twaddle, stuff and nonsense, bilge, balderdash and general poppycockery. I'm not superstitious. I'm not even slightly stitious.

Etiquette columns are full of queries from hosts who have accidentally invited twelve people to a dinner party, and want to dis-invite somebody to avoid having thirteen at the table. One English adviser suggested that the host go out after receiving his guests. (Why he couldn't just have invited somebody else and thrown another cup of water in the soup is anyone's guess.)

There is no denying fear of thirteen (triskaideka-phobia) crosses many cultures. According to an ancient *Brewer's Dictionary of Phrase and Fable*, the very word has been largely expunged from the Turkish language, the Italians never use the number in lotteries and Parisians avoid thirteen as a house number and have a special name for people who make up a fourteenth at dinner parties: Quartorziennes. Norse mythology says thirteen at dinner is unlucky, and Judas made up the thirteen at the Last Supper and abused the hospitality so comprehensively that he's still off everybody's party list after about 2000 years.

An expert on triskaidekaphobia (you knew there would be one, and if you thought they might be from America you get the cigar), Dr Thomas Fernsler, sits in an office at a uni in Pennsylvania mulling over the whole catastrophe. He thinks it might have something to do with maths—that twelve is a 'complete' number (twelve months, twelve zodiac signs, twelve labours of Hercules, although he doesn't mention twelve Brandy Alexanders before full poisoning occurs, resultant twelve-step programs etc) and therefore thirteen is just beyond complete and 'hence restless—so restless, in fact that it intersects *the realm of evil*'. Hey, that's pretty mathematical.

That quote from Dr Fernsler comes from the *Sunday Telegraph* in England, but unfortunately the article neglects to mention whether he's the dean of wacko maths or what. Anyway, the doc reckons when you combine the number of people at the Last Supper with the day that Jesus was crucified you get Friday the thirteenth.

The article goes on to urge you to consider also the Apollo 13 mission which was launched on 11 April 1970 (and if you add 4, 11 and 70 you get 85 and 8 and 5 is OH MY GOD 13) from launching pad 39 (3 times 13) at 13.13 local time and was blown up on 13 April. (I would consider it myself, but I have always found adding up to be unlucky for me.) Fernsler points out that US President Roosevelt was triskathingy-phobic, and he even died on a Thursday 12 April, avoiding Black Friday by a day, but clearly *almost* implicating himself in the Apollo 13 disaster in a very spooky way.

Dr Fernsler further explains that he once weighed himself (169 pounds—the 13th multiple of 13) before getting on a flight to Nashville which touched down at exactly 13.13 where he called for transport and was told to dial option 13 and then he delivered a maths paper in the lobby of his hotel because *a pipe had burst in the auditorium.* Dr Fernsler doesn't add that it's doubly unlucky for him that he is not a plumber, because fixing auditorium pipes is probably more lucrative than being a triskywhatsitphobia expert.

Neither did Dr Fernsler calculate that the Nashville pipe fiasco was in 1992 and if you add those numbers together you get 21 and if you add those together you get 3 which is just one less that the number 4 which is 1 and 3 added together and those are the exact same numbers that make up the number 13 and being one less than the soothing number 4 makes it not so much a restless number which brings it into *the realm of evil,* but a tedious number which brings us into *the realm of falling insensible to the floor in a miasma of boredom.* Have a nice day.

# OH MY GODDESS

Stuck in a lift recently all I had was an eyeliner pencil and a newspaper with an 'easy' crossword full of clues like 'Daughter of Hoosiebobulus, ruler of Poot. A righteous blonde (5 letters)'. Or 'Felloverus, a mymph of Obea who was changed into a small echidna until Zeus tweaked his leather thonging, making him the protector of the Smyrdian mutton wranglers (17 letters and three umlauts).'

Sick of finding that 'Craig' didn't fit, it seemed time, on my release, to purchase the very stout *Dictionary of Classical Mythology* by Pierre Grimal, published by Blackwell. But before we get to the myth of Camilla, a short word from ye olde 1990s.

Prince Charles is still trying to get Britain to accept that he, the head of a whole entire church, should be able to go on doing the hokey pokey in the nicky noo nar with a woman who is not his wife, because princes can jolly well do what they like, except be king. His consort, Camilla, is a horsey, outdoorsy, chain-smoky type.

In the classically mythical past, however, Camilla was a little princess escaping from soldiers with her dad, the king of the Volsci (not unlike the king of the Kombi only with fewer dreadlocks). Trapped, the king tied his little girl to a spear and hurled it across the river. (Which, along with boarding school, is the kind of high quality child care you can expect from royals, apparently.)

Anyway, the king promised that if Camilla survived, her life would be dedicated to (oh my GOD, this is sooooo, like, spooky…) Diana. Diana accepted the prayer and Camilla turned into a bit of an outdoorsy, horsey type galloping around the woods, pining for past princessery. Diana, of course, remained the contantly premenstrual bitchface goddess type.

It is hard not to look for modern parallels, especially because mythically classical times seemed to be full of sex, drugs, raunchy pan-pipe music, mad violence, illogical tantrums, child abuse, haruspication (fortune-telling by animal entrails), ludicrous plots (people getting pregnant from looking at fruit), bad hairdos (Medusa) and other 'Melrose Place'-style antics. There was Icarus who flew too close to the sun, Oedipus's mum who got too close to her son and now some politicians who flew too close to the wind, and messed with the travel allowance fairy.

Another ancient classical myth-type person is Gaia, who new-age types bang on about as the earth mother goddess. I had always pictured Gaia as a cross between Stevie Nicks and Jabba the Hut wearing a ratty old shawl, making her own stoneground underpants and beaming stupidly at her 567 children who would bring her sheaves of wheat and pomegranates she could sing about in a reedy way. It is astonishing to find that it is worse than that.

She urged her son to cut off his dad's testicles as he was about to have sex with her, and then she got pregnant from her husband's blood. The same son, slightly unhinged by now if you want a wild guess and also the ruler of the world, ate all his children except one, because Gaia fooled him into eating a stone instead, thinking it was his baby. (Could happen to anybody in a hurry.)

Later Gaia had it off with Tartarus, the god 'who personified the abyss of Hell'. Now, many of us have dysfunctional families, and most of us have had the odd one-night stand or affair with a total no-hoper rat-faced embarrassment we cringe to even think of when we're sober, but a person who officially had the gig of personifying the abyss of hell? Probably even had the uniform? How pissed would you have to be?

Gaia, far from being the benign earth mother of all creation, could have sustained a whole month of Oprah Winfrey shows and a self-help book called *We're Okay, She's a Barking Maniac*. Thanks for coming and sharing that with us, Gaia, honey. Mything you already.

# WITCHES, ANGELS AND
# CODPIECES AKIMBO

A glut of Jane Austen films, several movies with young men in grown men's bodies (like we don't get that in real life) and now—angels. When Hollywood gets a craze there's no stopping it. Angels in the outfield, angels on the telly and, hello, John Travolta as the eponymous Michael, an angel addicted to lollies and smokes.

I watched the angel show on the telly, 'Touched By an Angel', to learn that African-American boss angels eat meatballs and that the Angel of Death is a white guy called Andy, with a James Spader haircut, miraculous American teeth, a spivvy grandpa shirt, white waistcoat and camel overcoat. (If you see a man dressed like this, run away. He's either the Angel of Death or a total wanker.)

Denzel Washington plays an angel in *The Preacher's Wife*, imparting sweetness and light in a three-piece suit (clearly God has some kind of contra deal with Armani). It is an ineluctably attractive idea, being able to conjure up Denzel Washington but, as fantasies go, most people would rather he turned up with a swag of cash or at least some massage oil.

The latest word is that Dolly Parton is set to frock up as an angel in her next film and I think it might be worth it just to see the frocks. Thankfully Dolly has never gone easy on the sequins in nine-to-five wear. She is a shining beacon to all of us interested in shiny, expensive cack, never mind angels.

As legendary beings go, witches are another groove entirely. The herbalists of yesteryear, they were dumped on by the churches for interfering with God's will. 'Right. I see you've put a Middle Ages bandaid on this lad's leg. Into the village pond with you, missy.'

'Witches' were hounded, drowned, or burned at the stake because obviously their power came straight from the devil. There were several ways to recognise a witch, including being the owner of a cat or rat, and having facial moles (Cindy Crawford would have been lashed to a bunch of faggots as soon as look at her).

(Witches also ran into trouble as the joint barbers and surgeons' associations wanted the herbalists out of the way. Presumably you used to walk into a salon/clinic and the bloke on duty would ask if you wanted a moustache trim or your leg off.)

Hollywood has produced *The Witches of Eastwick*, a vehicle for Jack Nicholson's leer, and the current Arthur Miller film about persecution, *The Crucible*, with grumpy old Daniel Day Lewis, more Lear than leering.

The most famous telly witch was Samantha, in 'Bewitched', married to a dreary advertising executive. She used to cast spells by wrinkling her nose, but in keeping with 1950s values, her husband always tried to restrain her as a 'normal' housewife. Why she never turned him into a small ferret is a mystery.

The new telly one is 'Sabrina the Teenage Witch' in which Melissa Joan Hart sends the pert-ometer off the dial. She has a wisecracking black cat which looks like a cross between a mangy cat corpse with animatronics in it or one of those things with a stomach-zip to keep your shorty pyjamas in. Luckily for Melissa Joan her show could not possibly be as much of a turkey as *Sabrina* the film, which had Harrison Ford in ever decreasing circles lumbering around that simpering woman who was such a good actor she now sells perfume.

Some people believe in angels and some people believe themselves to be witches. But if Hollywood's keen on legend-inspired crazes, may we recommend 'Xena, Warrior Princess', filmed for TV in Auckland, Ancient Greece. None of this wussy angel business, or twitching her schnozz in a ladylike way. It's brass bosoms akimbo and in with a dirty great sword to conquer the scaly monster. Phwoaarr. Xena's rating the metal codpiece off her former squeeze, Hercules. Long may her immutable bosoms… um…immute.

# TO THE RESCUE

A friend carries a small vial of Rescue Remedy in her handbag for emergencies. You know, like a riot in Ouagadougou or breaking a fingernail or something. According to the pamphlet from the health food shop, Rescue Remedy is a 'mixture of five flower essences...a calming panacea...used in all sorts of stressful situations'.

I imagine it's very useful for, say, bank robberies:

'Every one of you fuckers! Down on the floor!'

'Excuse me young man, while I heal my negative emotions caused by this sudden shock by popping four droplets of Rescue Remedy in a glass of water and quaffing it slowly in order to alleviate the stress of this anxious event. Alternatively I might just let the drops dissolve underneath my tongue.'

'Jesus, Kev, let's do over the TAB instead.'

The pamphlet explains that apart from Rescue Remedy, there are thirty-eight other Bach flower remedies invented by Dr Edward Bach, who was a Harley Street, London, doctor, in case you thought he was a Harley Street, Byron Bay, doctor. His remedies for certain personality traits or 'undesired emotions', he reckoned, 'raise our vibrations and open up our channels for the reception of the spiritual self.' (Bach is pronounced as in 'barking', incidentally.)

Dr Bach, sadly, passed away before the word 'feral' was invented. But you can make up your own formula of essences. For example, if you are unsure of a path in life, desperate and suicidal, ruthless and inflexible, jealous AND dream of the future, you'll need a mixture of wild oat, cherry plum, vine, holly and clematis.

You pop all the flower essences into a dropper bottle and fill it with equal parts brandy and mineral water. It is significant that the pamphlet does not expressly forbid the immediate necking of the rest of the brandy, which might help when you are plagued by 'mental worry and torture but appear cheerful' if you don't fancy a few drops of centaury, whatever that is. Possibly a herb with hooves.

The unwanted emotions identified by Dr Bach are grouped under several subheadings: uncertainty, over-sensitivity, fear, loneliness, insufficient interest in present circumstances, despondency and despair, and overcare for others' welfare, which curiously includes 'emotions' such as self-denial and martyrdom, desire to dominate others and self-indulgence and self-pity. Perhaps Dr Bach was a nun-baiting disciplinarian. (Lucky for him he wasn't born in Australia: he probably would have been nicknamed 'Stringy'.)

One of the problems with Bach flower remedies is that there could be perfectly good reasons for 'desire to be alone' (Greta Garbo obviously shunned droplets of water violet) or 'repeatedly seeks advice from others' (no drops of cerato for the prime minister, thank you—although you might like to set up an intravenous drip of honeysuckle—for being absorbed in memories of the past).

The whole Helen Demidenko-Darville pants-pretty-much-constantly-on-fire business could be hosed down if somebody gave her a barrel of chicory to suck on (for demanding attention) and the High Court bench could be force-fed beech for being too judgmental. In fact, time for an aerial spraying of Canberra with chestnut bud (failure to learn from the past).

I'm sure working out a Bach flower remedy is kind of fun—like doing a horoscope, going to a psychic or doing a quiz in a women's magazine. ('Are you a fat idiot? Try our quiz and you'll feel like one!') Properly prescribed herbs can be powerful therapeutic agents, but four drops of cherry plum flower essence for being 'desperate and suicidal'? Get out of it. Oops, expectation of failure. I must go and immerse myself in a vat of larch.

# STAY OUT OF THE DRAGON'S BUM

Have you copped onto the *Woman's Day* feng shui column yet? Initially, one might find it a bit strange taking advice on an 'ancient Chinese wisdom' from someone called Selena Summers who is photographed wearing a cheong-sam dress, holding a parasol and a paper fan. But we are a multicultural nation. And no doubt she has spent years studying in Beijing.

Personally I don't think *Woman's Day* is really entering into the spirit of things enough. I think they could have had Selena standing on the Great Wall near a Ming vase, wearing a triangular hat, on a bicycle, with some wooden thongs on stilts, reading an Amy Tan book, waving some chopsticks and shouting, 'Let a thousand dissidents bloom!' With one of those baseball caps with a red star on the front. On top of the triangular hat.

My subconscious has just pointed out to me that some of my lovely readers may not know about the ancient Chinese wisdom of feng shui (pronounced: 'fung shway', or possibly 'obsessive interior decoration'). It is a set of rules regarding the harmonious arrangement of the geography of one's home. For example, one should not live in a shotgun shack as the back door is directly opposite the front door and hence energy entering the home can simply scoot straight out again, not unlike a visiting Mormon evangelist.

So, people write to Selena Summers, the ancient Chinese wise person, and ask things like 'Should I hang the budgie cage over the couch?' 'Is a mirror on the bedroom ceiling a good idea?' (unfortunately I've never actually seen that query) and also the odd relationship concern such as 'My fiancee, a Rat, is a pastry chef, while I am an excitable Dragon who owns a dress shop'.

Selena advises that they look for a peaceful home with water views where 'the two of you will live like a king and queen'. No doubt she'll be forthcoming next week on the best feng shui method of safe-cracking.

A. L. of Alice Springs writes that there is a hallway in her lounge room where the prosperity point should be. This is the kind of attention to detail shown by the owners of the Crown Fleecing Complex in Melbourne who had a feng shui expert help design the joint.

It was once reported that Siiiiimon Reynolds' advertising company HQ was designed along feng shui principles with executives at the head of a dragon shape, and lesser paid minions at desks (do not read on if offended by vulgarisms) up the dragon's arse.

Selena is full up to pussy's bow with handy hints. 'Gypsies,' says Selena, 'are usually healthy because they don't stay in any one place long enough to pick up bad energy.' Typhoid, maybe, but no bad energy. Well, I hope nobody tells Selena about Nazi concentration camps, or the constant struggle of modern gypsies to get medical attention from European governments. Perhaps she means the gypsies in Enid Blyton stories, who were always dirty and suspicious (being *foreign*, you understand) but fairly robust.

Selena also suggests that inner-city dwellers switch on garden lights most evenings. Mozzies must be tremendously good feng shui.

# 4
# Fashion
# &
# Phoofing

# THE DUMB FASHION AWARDS

We cannot let the year end without rustling the gussets of the fashion industry one last time. (A poster advertising a band called the Gusset Rustlers was torn down in a nearby street recently. Probably a disgruntled *Vogue* employee.)

First up, let us examine the field of the Body Police. There were women's magazines telling us to feel good about ourselves the way we are on page four and how to get thinner on all the other pages. There was the Trevor Hendy stomach-crunching thingie, which looked remarkable like the Jane Flemming stomach-crunching thingie, both sold by people on daytime telly who looked like they'd had a pert overdose and who disapproved of our tummies.

But the winner of the *Body Police Mind Your Own Parts Buster Award* is (trumpet blurt, thank you Mervyn) Mr Osmel Souza, the former frock designer who chooses the contestants for Miss Venezuela—the country which has, in the past seventeen years, blitzed the competition by winning five Miss Worlds and four Miss Universe titles (as alert readers will recall, Miss Universe is harder to win because people from other planets may enter).

We are indebted to a report in the *Economist* magazine about Mr Souza, who tootles around Venezuela with a team of perving assistants, trawling through 'discotheques, shopping centres, schools, and…the street' for girls or women who fit the bill.

The bill to fit is as follows: aged seventeen to twenty-four, educated (to answer questions on the podium), at least 1.7 metres tall (5'7"). Once the list has been narrowed down, the girls or women are inspected in swimsuits by Mr Souza and his assembled pervs (that's the women in swimsuits, not the pervs, natch), who are mostly cosmetic and dental surgeons. 'Technicians' then assess the would-be contestant for body-fat percentage, cellulite, and what surgery Mr Souza's team orders for them: eyebrows, noses, chins, breasts and teeth are common targets.

The official team dentist, Mr Moises Kaswan, told the *Economist* some young women have their gums painfully retracted to show 'Farrah Fawcett teeth, toilet-bowl white'. Yummo. The girls or women are chosen early, in the hope that their physical scars, swelling, possible complications and bruising will heal before the contest.

'A woman has to strike me like a blow,' says Mr Souza. Personally, I'd be glad to oblige.

Okay, and now on to the *Dumb As Toast Fashion Idea of the Year Award* (the envelope please, Mervyn—love those lederhosen, babe). And the winner is: bum cleavage! Yes, those brainy designers came up with a brilliant idea to make frocks with holes cut in the very lower back area, to show the first few centimetres of what is known in the glamorous world of haute couture as 'bum crack' or, as we know it in Australia, the land of low-slung elasticised shorts—'the Builder's Smile'. It was recommended as the perfect look for a job interview, or picking the kids up from school (or maybe that part was a hallucination) and real women everywhere have flocked so far away from it there's been a change in the Earth's axis.

An English reporter for the *Guardian* newspaper recently reported that ten years ago the frock-maker Galliano remarked in conversation that he didn't like bosoms because they spoil the line of a frock. Mr Galliano, now head of the House of Dior, a man who would rather women looked like a bit of four-by-two for draping reasons, made the $150,000 nightie which Princess Diana wore to a ball in New York.

And so (Mervyn, raise your goblet and adjust your jerkin bodice) we toast the winner of the *I'm So Miserable I'd Like to Cheer Myself up by Running around Practically in the Nicky Noo Nar But I Can't Be Stuffed So I'll Settle for a Petticoat in Public Award*, Mrs Beryl Biffo of Mount Druitt. What a shame nobody asked her to the ball.

# THE INNER NANNA DIET

Hands up everyone on some kind of ludicrous post-Christmas short-term diet involving tubes of pineapple extract or all eggs one day, sardine juice the next? Well stop it. You'll only get hungry and cranky.

Just eat less fat, and more of the kind of green stuff that isn't lime-flavoured extruded food dye and get your heart rate up for more than half an hour more than three times a week.

Don't panic about the number of mince pies you ate or forbid yourself certain foods, because you will crave those particular foods with an intensity that exceeds even patriotism, mother-love and the compelling desire to poke Senator Nick Minchin in the eyes with a stick. (To test this out, I recently forbade myself chocolate and then had to move into the Cadbury factory armed only with a disposable lighter and a funnel.)

But panic people do, and don't the marketing people and the more whim-whammed diet advisers know it. There is nothing new to say except move around more and don't eat so much crap. This does not stop them.

In one magazine recently a woman who eats her toddler's leftovers was told to spray the remaining food with flyspray or Windex or something so she couldn't polish it off. That sibilant whirling sound is every grain of my Nanna's ashes trying to turn in their grave. (What on earth does 'turn in the grave' actually mean, anyway?)

I digress, which probably means I'm channelling Nanna.

She could have digressed for the Olympics and given the dais a polish while the national anthem was on, but there I go again. Nanna was of the firm belief that no food was to be wasted—it either went to the chooks, the dogs, the garden, or the leftovers (being one of Nan's five food groups, along with meat, sponges, pav and Tarzan jubes).

And then (astonishingly enough in the United States of America) they came up with a 'fat-free' oil which basically was some description of oil which did not have fat in it but had the unfortunate side-effect of not necessarily being absorbed by the body—the body, quite sensibly, going, 'Gawd, what's this weird stuff? Toxic waste? Can't think of a thing to do with it. Dispatch!' This was delicately described in some literature as 'anal leakage'.

The manufacturers must know that there are some people so desperate to be thinner they'll even put up with the horizontal squirts if they think they're going to have the body of a prepubescent person without actually being prepubescent. Fat chance.

And now, from another magazine, the revelation that someone in novelty marketing is faffing about with a plastic container full of dirt called Diet Dirt. You're supposed to throw some onto your dinner so you don't eat it.

I'm thinking of developing a new product myself. Called 'Listen to Your Inner Nanna', it's a series of subliminal tapes which constantly feed certain phrases to your brain while you're asleep. Such as 'Take a long hard look at y'self my girl' and 'What a load of flamin' codswallop' and 'Have another scone, it won't bite'.

# THE FIVE STYLES OF FASHION

There are only five styles of fashion. They come and go but are known by different names so that the fasho industry can con us into thinking we need about five zillion dollars worth of NEW clothes every 'season'. As a community service we present (trumpeting elephant noises)…THE FIVE STYLES OF FASHION! Hurrah! Darling! Smooch! It's divine! To die for! (*Do* go on.)

## 1. TOO, TOO GLAMOROUS
Also known as yuppie, evening wear, or sexy. It's dark red lippy, three kilos of mascara, long frocks (gowns), cleavage, gloves, velvets, silks, stockings, black, red, purple, hair up but still kinda tousled and tumbly and wrangled by professionals, lingerie and plenty of it, and flashy jewellery or real jewellery. In a nutshell: expensive as all get out.

## 2. BLOODY BORING
Also known as classic, essential, preppy, back-to-basics, Sloane Ranger. Anything in navy, particularly one strand of pretendy pearls, men in moleskins and business shirts, plenty of cardies, loafers (meaning shoes, not the idle rich) Peter Pan collars and ankle-length pleated skirts (only a small Toyota up your left nostril is less flattering).

## 3. ALLEGEDLY 'FEMININE'
Also known as 'baby doll' dresses, fifties style, girly, or don't make me vomit. Flouncy, fluffy, frou-frou frippery, diaphanous, lacy, pinks, pastels, hair ribbons, pig tails, plaits,

patent leather shoes, ankle socks, simpering, sucking on lollipops in the magazine photographs like wanton three-year-olds, you know the sort of generally offensive caper. Very strappy, high-heeled shoes also qualify, as corsetry and hopeless tottering are supposed to indicate helplessness and a certain alluring feminine sexual something, i.e. I'm so dumb I can't walk straight.

## 4. COMPLETE CRAP

Also known as punk, grunge, street, real, recession chic, homeless style, junkie fashion, drug dreck, etc. Basically horrible clothes in unnatural fabrics which look unkempt, dirty, ripped, stained, ill-fitting, holey, back to front. The flash designers will put out this same stuff with thousand-dollar labels on it. Also nasty little unnatural fabrics with a mean amount of material, for example skirts the size of matchboxes with a size 16 label on them.

## 5. THE UNWEARABLE

On the catwalk this means see-through T-shirts for work, topless office wear, anything by Thierry Mugler, anything by a new designer trying to break into the scene, anything by an old designer totally out of ideas, Vivienne Westwood's false botties, those insane make-up disasters with glitter all over the face or twigs sticking out of your eyebrows with orange eyeshadow and green lipstick. Off the catwalk we are talking hobble skirts too tight to stride in, bubble skirts too bouffy to sit in, platform shoes you can't walk in without life-long ankle injury, padded and hoisted bras too tight to be composed in, and tights too unnatural to avoid thrush in.

This also works with colours. They change every 'season' so you think you need a new lot. The five colour groups that recycle (usually in this order) are Pastels (also known as gelati, pales, iced colours: these make everyone look like they are ice-cream vendors); Brights (aka: fluorescents, citrus, these usually look hideous on everybody except Somalis); Naturals (aka: beige, sand, beige, beige and camel: this can look like it's bandicoot camouflage season at David Jones); Combo (aka a fad for stripes, polka dots, florals, plaids or paisley); or finally Classics (black, brown is the new black, navy is the new brown: this means you get to choose between Morticia Addams and Bronwyn Bishop).

PS: While you're debriefing, stick with the companies which have signed the Fairwear agreement to pay properly their home-sewing workers. They include Target, Country Road, Witchery, Just Jeans, Jacqui E, Ken Done, King Gee, Najee, Sara Lee (get that cheesecake off your head), Intimates, Peter Weiss, Sport Fashion, Sportsgirl, Sportcraft and Cue Design.

# SAUCY SCARLET SHEILA CLOBBER

There is a furore or possibly a brouhaha or maybe even a kerfuffle over the fact that 'Sale of the Century' co-host Nicky Buckley is flaunting her disgracefully pregnant self on the telly.

Miss Buckley's crime, according to critics, many of them called Enid and approximately 157 years old, is not hiding her pregnancy underneath more decorous outfits: for example a bottle-green doona cover, Islamic robes, or an attractive accessorised tarpaulin.

Meanwhile, Miss Buckley is continuing to wear sexy slinky strappy saucy slippery skintight shameful devil-baiting slut-featured scarlet sheila peekaboo huzzy wanton gowns which fail to disguise the fact that at some point she has probably taken part in an act of sexual congress. The JEZEBEL!

I'll tell you one thing for free, it'd be a damn sight worse if men could get pregnant. There's be no stopping them. Newsreaders breastfeeding on air, and Ray Martin looking straight into the camera and saying, 'Goodnight viewers—and by the way, I'm doing my pelvic floor exercises RIGHT NOW.' That weather guy would have a special pointer on the ABC every night at 7.25 to indicate his uterine contractions.

But back to the unholy flaunting jezebel witch. Perhaps some special legislation could be brought in by Senator Harradine, himself 152 years old, from that great bastion of progressive views, Tasmania. Nicky Buckley should be clapped in chains and forced into a small cardboard box until her time is nigh. I mean pregnancy used to be called a confinement and why not? What could be more unnatural than getting pregnant! Off with her head!

And if it's a matter of whether the frocks are tasteful—hello! This is 'Sale of the Century' we're talking about!

## CHANNEL SEVEN NEWS, SORT OF

Tonight there's a Channel Seven news special on how to be wrinkle free. And I think that's the kind of thrilling, hard-hitting factual journalism that makes us proud to be in the information profession.

People are having injections which plump out the wrinkles—often it's fat from other areas of the body, so the expression 'arse face' takes on a whole new meaning.

Some American women have injections into their frown lines—so they literally can't frown. Their faces are frozen into a bland stupid expression not unlike those catwalk models who seem to be tranquilised with a stun-gun in between outfits.

Of course you can do this at home by injecting any old substance into your face—sump oil, margarine, small pets around the house. But remember—be *safe*—don't share needles.

# A Marvy Makeover

Remember those magazine articles which told you to get together with a girlfriend and spend a whole day in a face mask, doing your toenails and playing with your hair? This is the revised version.

**7 am:** Are you insane? What are you doing up? Get back to bed.

**9 am:** Don't be ridiculous.

**10 am:** Open one eye and moan piteously.

**10.30 am:** Normally you'd be advised to begin the day with a glass of water with lemon juice in it. Pish tosh. Bribe a reliable local child to go to the nearest coffee shop and get you a very strong coffee indeed, about five croissants, a cherry Danish and a few sausages.

By this time you should have stocked the fridge with vodka, coffee, most of the chocolate biscuit brands known to humankind, and some creamy custard yoghurt. Lock all fresh fruit, vegetables and tofu in a strongbox. (Incidentally, if the local child is your own offspring, this is the time to bribe them to go somewhere else for the day, preferably Venezuela.)

**11 am:** Get a basin with ice in it (ice is very good for early morning eye puffiness), an eyelash curler and a lemon. While perusing the telly guide grasp the eyelash curler tongs firmly in your right hand, use them to grasp some ice and drop the ice carefully into a stiff gin and tonic. Place an elegant slice of the lemon into the glass.

**11.07 am:** Place the video remote control within easy

reach. We'll be doing some arm lifts with that later. Greet your friend who has just arrived and make her a G and T.

**11.15 am:** Now is the time for some relaxing aroma-therapy—if it seems absolutely necessary, you may put the garbage out.

**11.20 am:** Moisturising. Either you can buy some scientific-looking vials of anti-ageing liposome unsaponifiable non-comedogenic hydroacidic vegetable protein bovine placenta and French plankton extract free-radical taunting body treatment business at approximately $14,000 a gram and slather it all over your entire body, OR you could just put some olive oil on your knees, which will be very tiring indeed, and you will probably have to take a lie down almost immediately. Both of you could stare at the corners of the ceiling for, say, half an hour or so, wondering if those cobwebs pre-date the Middle Ages.

**11.45 am:** Now it's time to attend to your furry bits. Shampoo and style the hair on your legs. Check to see whether or not your underarm hair might make a plait. Now, facial hair. If you have developed quite a full moustache, you might like to consider waxing. One of those jaunty moustaches which curl up at the ends like the ones on the Three Musketeers might be nice. Take some warm wax in your fingertips and shape the ends of your moustache into a nice kiss-curl.

By this time you should be at least part way through any of the following videos: *An Affair to Remember; Clueless; The Big Easy.* If you or your friend have any supermodel exercise videos and an exercise bike, this would be a good time to jam the video in between a vital piece of machinery and the wheel.

**1 pm:** Lunch. And plenty of it. Be sure to take something from each of the five food groups: caffeine, chocolate, biscuitry, fruit custard flan and popcorn.

**1.45 pm:** You may care to clean your teeth thoroughly with an oscillating electric toothbrush, floss every crevice, gargle with mouthwash and paint them with plaque-frightener. Or not. Not is fine.

**2 pm:** Time to do your hair. Usually a magazine will suggest the following: 'Wash the hair carefully with a very expensive shampoo at least eight times. Condition, and rinse. Repeat. Apply hot-oil treatment. Wash hair again (as above). Heat a thick towel in the microwave to wrap around your head after you have coloured it with about three separate colour treatments, pausing between each one to cover your head in clingwrap. (Leave nostril holes.)

'Put the hair in heated rollers. Use curling enhancer and a fair bit of tong work for finishing touch and roll hair into a French pleat topknot bob bun with tendril involvement. Now apply some volume root lift spray putty grease amplifying tonic fudge gel mousse laminate varnish gloss and fingerstyle vigorously while drying with a hairdryer of approximately 38,000 watts. Add any accessories such as jauntily placed sunglasses, a bunch of tulips, a tiara or an attractive, battery-operated Alice band.'

Personally, girls, I'd give it all a miss and just pop on the tiara.

By this time, any of the following videos should have been started: *Thelma and Louise; All About Eve; The Women;*

or if you want to end up enjoying a huge, soggy, snorking, mascara-detonating sob, try *Running on Empty*. Eat five Tim Tams each.

**2.30 pm:** Cellulite check. Put on some loud music, give it all a waggle about and do the Buttock Fling. Ten points to each girlfriend who can make their buttocks clap together with a good hearty rhythmic 'fwack!'

**2.50 pm:** How completely exhausting. Lower yourself into a lovely bubble bath and stay there reading a stack of (a) obvious trash (e.g. Barbara Cartland) or (b) less obvious trash. Stay in the bath until (a) your skin looks like Barbara Cartland's or (b) you fall asleep and nearly drown. Pop on another nightie, or perhaps a singlet and Cottontails. Don't worry—you're not going to answer the door, because it's time for the mask.

**5.30 pm:** *The Mask*. But if you're not a Jim Carrey fan, any other video will do. Pop some cucumber slices on your eyes during the video piracy warning and then make cucumber sandwiches and scones.

**6 pm:** Give yourself a pedicure and manicure including a cuticle push, buff, polish, file, nail-hardener, top coat and bottom coat, and don't forget to prop your toenails apart with wads of cottonwool balls or Tim Tams. Alternatively, just give all twenty nails a quick trim around the edges with your teeth or a Stanley knife.

**7.30 pm:** Time to pay attention to your pectorals, thigh muscles, hamstrings, abs, flabs, arms, ankles, and buttock-ulor region. Greet them all individually and ask them if they've had a nice day. I imagine they'd care to watch a Cary Grant/Katharine Hepburn video.

**8 pm:** Dinner. The most important meal of the day. You may have, in the following order: one serve of ice-cream; three serves of toast; twelve serves of carbohydrates and the leafy bits of the top of a stick of celery. For maximum effect, the leafy bits should be shoved in the top of a Bloody Mary. Get stuck into the rest of the vodka.

**9.30 pm:** Sea shanties.

**10 pm:** Pass out on couch. Friends may pass out on floor.

**4.30 am:** Smell burning. Remove thick towel from microwave.

# FALSE BOSOMS AHOY

I bought my false boosies from K-Mart, where it's all very cloak and dagger, kind of like one of those old spy films where everybody talks in code. You go to the lingerie section, then you take the empty box from the shelf to the fragrance section and the perfume girls put your bosoms in a box.

I had a bit of a goss with the girls and apparently the bosoms have been walking out the door, so now they're a big ticket anti-shoplifting under-the-counter option.

I said, 'I'm just buying these false bosoms because I'm going to be talking about them on the Martin–Molloy radio show.'

She rolled her eyes. 'That's what they all say.'

Although apparently the majority of false bosoms have been sold to women to wear at their own wedding.

And I just want to warn any blokes out there that if, in a haze of post-wedding piss-up you reach fondly for your new life-partner and a boosie comes off in your hand, do not under any circumstances scream the house down. What you may have found is a K-Mart boosie. Which is kind of like cold congealed custard in a bag with a false nipple on the front. (They flop around with the energy of a dead mullet.)

Girls: Don't buy these things. They're stupid. Plus, you need to buy a bra two cup sizes bigger and then you stuff it full of what looks like a sullen jellyfish with second stage rigor mortis. I mean you might as well put a couple of packets of frozen peas down your singlet and call it erotica.

# MORE BOSOMS ALERT

I don't know whether anyone's noticed but the star of the 'X-Files' Gillian Anderson was showing a nipple at the Golden Globe Awards. She was wearing a low-cut dress and oopsy narna—out popped a nipple in full view.

Why this never happens with blokes I have no idea. Maybe they have major event zipper monitors who go around checking that there are no al fresco lunch boxes—I can't say.

Now if I could just escape into history for a minute: Gillian appears to be reviving a nineteenth-century trend where evening gowns were so low cut that they just cut across the middle of the nipple, showing the top half. This was tremendously entertaining until Queen Victoria put a stop to that sort of behaviour by dressing in a black tarpaulin and a dirty great tiara for the next 1200 years. This outfit became known as The Black Death.

Anyway, back to bosoms.

*Vogue* recently reported that a fashion trend was for visible erect nipples under your outfit—otherwise known as headlights or party hats. For example at last year's Academy Awards the following actresses had visible nipples: Whoopi, Nicole Kidman, Goldie Hawn, Jessica Lange, Naomi Campbell (I don't know what she's doing in this list of actresses), Alicia Silverstone, Anjelica Huston, Winona Ryder and—brace yourself for a bit of a shock—Sharon Stone.

Ladies—I have two words to say to you all—gaffer tape.

And the last fashion trend is the new 'figure enhancing' pantyhose you can buy at Target called Shaper, which—how can I put this—allegedly hoists up your bum and packs it into a more elevated silhouette. In other words it is a buttock Wonder Bra. Personally, I can't see how it would work without some cables and a pulley system, but maybe that's just me.

# PHWOARR, CHECK OUT HER TEA TOWELS

One has noticed in one's local boutiquey area some natty miniskirts made of tea towels. Clearly a tremendously fun idea for those among us who plan never to wear a miniskirt again without being forced at gunpoint. (Likewise go-go boots, sparkly blue eyeshadow, the startled pomeranian perm, knock-off perfume ordered over the internet and nylon underdunders.)

(One also clocked in the shop a load of useless clothes the size of Hollywood actresses who are now so skinny their publicity shots are not taken dead front-on, because their heads look too thin. These poor algae-fed actrines will soon look like supportive, startled praying mantises with false bosoms.)

Anyway, there was also heaps of clobbair made from dyed chenille bedspread material (this is probably a sign that crocheted frocks are coming back). Taking a leaf from Aunty Benzo, one's mum used to boil up a huge copper on the stove and dye old bedspreads from the op-shop and then make us tracksuits with these tufty wavy lines on them, or, in the case of the all-over tufty, furry chenille look, one would leave the house looking like a gigantic, deranged aqua-go-green Muppet. One effortlessly recalls a purple tracksuit of this shag pile-style chenille which made people laugh out loud on sight.

A column in a local newspaper recently advised the skittish parents of a teenager who liked to wear tight clothes, miniskirts and crop-tops which showed her tummy. The adviser suggested the girl be warned that older men in particular might think this meant the girl wanted to have sex with them and she should read Helen Garner's book *The First Stone* to see how this could work out.

May one offer an alternative interpretation? If you're really worried about your daughter being assaulted or having consensual sex with any old hoon, suggest self-defence classes, acquaint her with her legal rights, tell her not to get legless drunk when she's out and always to travel in roaming packs of pals, help her develop a sassy, informed demeanour and wide interests, love her and make her love herself enough not to crave any old thing resembling affection, keep your fingers crossed and let her wear what she wants, even if it's half a tea towel.

Otherwise she's only going to change as soon as she gets to Janelle's place.

Sadly, there is a breed of chap characterised by neurons arranged in such a way for him to assume that any female with a pulse is dying to have sex with him, even if she's wearing a neck-to-knee shag-pile Muppet suit with furry epaulettes and moccasins.

One has bad news for any men who think that a young girl wearing a crop-top and a miniskirt means she wants to have sex with them. It just means she wants to wear a miniskirt and a crop-top. Especially if it drives the olds spare. But sex with an older man? Sorry, nah.

As a teen goddess said in a cafe the other day: 'I mean, the guy was ANCIENT. He must have been like THIRTY.' And all the other girls went: 'Eeeeuuuuwwwww.'

# DRIPPY LIPPIES

Fancy a lipstick shade called Mildew, Bruise or Plague? How about Oilslick (a black base with a rainbow sheen), Asphixia (lavender with a blue sheen) or Roach (dark shiny brown with a golden sheen)? What more can you expect from a cosmetics company called Urban Decay, with a grungier-than-grunge slogan like 'Does Pink Make You Puke?'

You can expect lipsticks or nail polish called Uzi (gunmetal colour), Frostbite, Smog (deep olive colour with coppery sheen), and something Marie Curie finally realised was a colour to die for, Radium (brilliant blue with a blue sheen). For the dissipated violets amongst us, the elegantly simple choice is obviously Pallor ('a light grey-green with a flesh coloured sheen')—but it doesn't say in the brochure whether the flesh colour more accurately represents Baby Spice or somebody from Bougainville. (I'll give you three guesses.)

With a fatalistic nod to the environment, Urban Decay also offers UVB lipstick (blue with lavender sheen) to represent UVB rays, a prime suspect in skin cancer cases, and Ozone clear nail polish and lip moisturiser, to 'protect'. (Presumably on the principle that if you have to get skin cancer, poppet, you may as well have nice nails when you wave goodbye.)

Urban Decay is run by Sandy Lerner, who told the *New York Times* last year, 'You can conform and have your little tantrum at the same time…A lot of investment bankers I know could lower their blood pressure 20 to 30 points if they had green fingernails.' Did you spot the creative, non-conformist, wild and crazy traits that will make Ms Lerner a financial success? That's right: she knows a lot of investment bankers.

Ms Lerner further informed that she used to be a computer networking inventor, and took away $200 million and her husband when they were bought out of their company in the late 1980s. She bought a Harley, and an English mansion owned by Jane Austen's brother (before he carked it) which she plans to turn into a centre for research into eighteenth- and nineteenth-century novelists. The woman has girly feminist cred coming out of her ears—and, presumably, mould on her lips.

Sadly, you can't actually buy her lippy in Australia yet, but you could possibly recreate the colours by mixing non-toxic fencing paint and colours from other ranges of lipsticks, which get along with names like 'Baby Doll', 'Hyacinth' and 'Kiss Kiss Noisette' (to itemise the contents of one's own handbag) but never seem to be called 'Sort of Pinky Reddish' or 'Cat's Bum Brown'.

US celebrities seem to be ignoring the Urban Decay lead, if you don't count Republicans who could well be wearing Pallor, or possibly Asphixia on bad days. According to a less-than-riveting lipstick page on the internet, actrine Drew Barrymore wears Chanel's Vamp (which would be called Dried Blood if Ms Lerner made it), Susan Sarandon wears Bobbi Brown's Nude (saucy minx) and Cindy Crawford claims to use Revlon's Pure Red, probably especially when she's being photographed in those Revlon ads for Pure Red lipstick. (Revlon must have a small Creative Naming Department, probably somebody called Candiii.)

It is obviously important to the future happiness of the global community that it becomes widely known that Tori Spelling uses Spice lipliner, Nancy Sinatra goes the 'Bardot' and Heather Locklear uses anything in a beige. So to speak.

Australian entrepreneur Poppy King was the first to get smart naming lipsticks, including Integrity, Ambition, Courage, Virtue, Liberty, Honesty, Faith, Hope, Charity, Lust, Avarice, Indolence, Vanity and rest of the seven deadly sins. The hot lipstick brand in the US, M.A.C. followed suit with names like Viva Glam, Verve and Captive (eh?).

But in light of the honesty displayed by the Urban Decay mob, it's probably time for Poppy to launch lipsticks called Slattern, Check-Out Chick, and Hard-Faced Socialite. Even more specific lippies could be produced, like Shut Up and Drive, Just Retrenched and Pre-Menstrual Tension Alert.

Believe me, there's a market.

# How to Get Dressed

Some advice to businesswomen who do not know how to dress themselves caught the eye recently. The handy hints of a consultant called Janine McMaster of Passion for Fashion Image Management are tremendously useful in themselves. Allow me to slightly elucidate her important points.

'SIMPLICITY IS BEST. YOU SHOULD NEVER HAVE A FULL WARDROBE.'

This means you. If your wardrobe is full, then set some small explosive charges at the bottom of the wardrobe to spur you on to a more empty wardrobe look. When in doubt, throw away all your clothes and have in your wardrobe only a little black dress and a pair of sturdy gumboots.

'AVOID DROP EARRINGS. THEY TEND TO DISTRACT PEOPLE WHEN YOU ARE TALKING.'

Especially toddlers, the mentally challenged, and the type of business executive who has tired of staring at your boosies when you talk.

'ANYONE CAN WEAR A LONG OR A SHORT SKIRT. SUCCESS DEPENDS ON REVEALING THE CURVE OF THE LEG.'

If your legs do not have any curves, draw some on with an eyebrow pencil. Long skirts are very useful because you can go straight from work to starring in an amateur theatrical production of 'Dr Quinn, Medicine Woman', or directly home to your Amish farm to do some quilting and making the sandwiches for a barn raising. Weeny skirts are terrific in an office situation, especially the ones the size of a Polish postage stamp, and especially if you spend your working week gouging out the insides of tuna or climb up ladders a lot.

'BRIEFCASES SHOULD NOT BE TOO BOXY OR MASCULINE AND DON'T CLUTTER YOUR IMAGE BY CARRYING A HAND-BAG AND A BRIEFCASE.'

No indeed. Nothing could be more offensive. Simply carry a feminine briefcase, preferably made from lacy baby-pink gingham with a big bow, and the items which you usually carry in a handbag such as money and tampons should be gaffer-taped to your forehead. In extreme cases, in which your work accoutrements take up a great deal of space, dispense with handbags and pesky masculine briefcases altogether and just push it all around in a shopping trolley you've nicked from Coles New World. Very feminine.

'MAKE-UP IS MEANT TO ENHANCE AND SHOULD BE NATURAL-LOOKING (RESEARCH HAS SHOWN THAT WOMEN WHO WEAR MAKE-UP EARN 25 PER CENT MORE THAN THOSE WHO DON'T).'

A very confusing statistic, given that men, who as a rule don't wear any make-up at all, consistently earn more than women. How very puzzling. Anyway, yes, and you can't go too far. One very natural look is to shave off the eyebrows entirely and then stick on some curvy black ones cut from a piece of Fuzzy Felt.

'DON'T WEAR ANYTHING TOO TIGHT OR ILL-FITTING.'
Here's an easy way to judge. If you can't move your legs, you might like to go up a size.

'INVEST IN ACCESSORIES. GOOD QUALITY SHOES, HAND-BAGS, BELTS AND SCARVES ALL CHANGE THE LOOK OF AN OUTFIT.'
In fact, with some practice, I think you'll find there's no need for an outfit at all. Just wear a good quality handbag, a scarf, a belt and some shoes and wait for those respectful comments and a promotion to come your way.

# BUTTOCK REMOVAL ALERT

A lot more holey moley than hotsy totsy. The *Australian* reports today that the look for spring/summer is going to be figure-hugging and sexy and we all need to diet. Brilliant. Don't suggest that the designers make clothes bigger than a size 4, just bang on about how we have to change— after all, we're the ones paying for the clothes.

Then the reporter Edith Lederer goes on to say 'the entire collection was skin tight, revealing bulges even on the models', in which case I think we'll have to take steps. Women clearly should not bulge anywhere. In fact, they should all look like curtain rods when they're lying down and a walking stick when they're standing up.

Right. Now to achieve this groovy new look, girls, I suggest we all have a bottom removal, get some detachable bosoms, and starve ourselves to death. Good on you, Edith, you big dork.

And true to form one of the designers showed bikini shorts, twenty-centimetre platform shoes, and shirts with sleeves made from socks with the heel pointing out. Just the thing to impress the boss, girls. And ladies at home— there's something for you, too, how about a sex-kitten leather outfit with plunging necklines and skirts just covering the bottom? That's if you want your bottom covered, I can't imagine why. All this from the label Red of Dead which two years ago had the catwalk models licking blood-stained scissors. Shriek chic.

# TAKE A HINT

There was a beauty hint in the paper recently that rather brought me up short. If you cannot wait for your nail polish to dry, advised the investigative journalist concerned, PLUNGE THE TIPS OF YOUR FINGERS INTO SOME OLIVE OIL.

And then, presumably, spend five hours getting the olive oil off your hands, your frock, the floor, next door's divan set, the letter box, your suede pumps, passers-by, the cook, the thief, his wife and the ceiling, and the tea towel collection you used in the process.

Just in case, I have set up a few areas around the house with buckets of olive oil. Really, I'm willing to learn. My former ignorance of this handy hint sent me to the latest fashion magazines to see what else I could be doing in those long hours spent thinking of my cuticles.

English *Vogue* was very useful: there is liquid gold eyeliner for grown-ups and cockroach-coloured nail polish for teenagers. Further reading revealed that at the hilariously named Lancôme Beauty Institute in Paris, 'girls as young as 10 or 11 are invited to come on Wednesday afternoons—when there is a half day (holiday) at school—for free—for lessons about scent, make-up and, above all, skin care.' (What can one learn about scent? It's not a suppository?) 'It seems to me,' foofed the *Vogue* journalist, 'that British teenagers could do with more of this kind of education.' And how *darling* of Lancôme not to charge for their indoctrination sessions.

Here's another grouse *Vogue* beauty hint: only dermatologists or surgeons should perform liposuction or any procedure which involves an incision or lasers. So, if you were thinking of getting a carpenter to remove your nipples and re-boot your entrails, cancel that booking.

Incidentally, the very same issue of *Vogue* carries a feature about cosmetics which look like food, for example Lady Primrose's Royal Extract Bathing Gel in a honey pot. (Lady Primrose might be onto something. Selling Extract of Royal might be a good solution to a family that otherwise just soaks up public money.)

There's a Prairie Hydra's Swiss moisturiser with—get this—caviar in it. Which explains why all the models in the same magazine look like they've got malnutrition: they've popped on some eyebrow pencil in the mistaken belief it was a three-course meal.

The first issue of *Vive!* in-flight magazine recommends 'Ella Baché Creme Intex No. 2 ($36.00)…a product no woman should be without. Powerful enough to get rid of the occasional breakout or ingrown hair by the time you touch down, it's simply brilliant.' Now, a lot of thought has gone into this, but it still remains a mystery—what do you reckon Creme Intex No. 2 might actually be? Sandpaper? Some kind of toxic waste? A prison-issue firearm with methylated spirits attachment?

On a rouge bent, *New Woman* reminds us to 'blow excess powder from the brush before you hit the cheeks'. Much better to get it in your eyes than on the wrong cheek bit. Also, the secret to avoiding puffy eyes is 'Sleep with your head elevated, avoid salt and alcohol'. So do try to cut down on eating fish and chips, getting pissed or lying down in your sleep.

It says you can also use Princess Marcella Borghese Botanico Eye Compresses. (Whoever Princess Marcella Borghese Botanico Eye is, possibly some distant relative of Prince Leonard of Hutt.) The compresses are $85, or you could use teabags but do be careful. It's very hard to get the gist of this beauty hint business as a beginner, and some of us are finding it a strain.

The well-known and internationally acclaimed head waxer, beauty therapiste and lifestyle adviser, Francine Panto (Miss) is constantly counselling people who didn't let the teabags cool down first. But, as Miss Francine says, you have to suffer to be beautiful.

# 5
# Haughty
# Culture

# LOIN DANCING

There was a thing on the telly the other night about a new modern dance company. The new director of the company was young for a government subsidised head of everything—under 437 years old, in fact. The reporter said he was so young and groovy that he watched the telly all the time to inspire his choreography.

Then they showed some footage of his choreography in action, to illustrate how fresh and modern and different and ground-breaking The Work is. Well, it was obvious that he'd watched 'Melrose Place', 'ER' and ads for Berlei pantery and brazzierrery, but I suspect he may also read *Vanity Fair*, in which all the celebrity blokes wear suits and all of the celebrity chicks are in their undies.

Much of The Work involved blokes in white coats menacing a whole lot of chicks hurling themselves about in lingerie. Tell a lie, there were some others dancing with no blokes, and chicks wearing a different sort of lingerie. (This is known in the trade as 'range'.)

Well, it's unfair to judge, really. There was no doubt a perfectly good reason why a whole bunch of girlies were hurling themselves around dressed in suspenders and silk knickers. Like, probably it was saying that the media would rather broadcast norks than talk about what the art is supposed to be saying. Which, in this case, is 'here are some norks to broadcast'. Post-modern, ay.

Once I attended a dance performance on a first date. (Whoops.) In the foyer afterwards, we met his friends.

'Mother of God,' said one, and for a second there I warmed to him. 'The entire narratived virginal sub-ether! The juxtaposition of the muscular central scream of art-fractioned willa-wolla bing-bong thought, surely?'

I asked stuff like, 'Was there a verb in that sentence?' and 'Who was the girl in the Heidi outfit and what did she have to do with Marie Antoinette, again?'

'Totally,' said somebody called Tristiniia.

Perhaps it is all very simple. As Aunty Ivy used to say, 'Modern dance is just people who can't act running around in the nuddy.' Unfair old cow. There's a fantastic, modern dance group in Australia called de Soxy. They often perform in Cottontails or long johns (now that's your Aussie lingerie) and do amazing things with their bodies and make you feel and think, just by looking at them move.

The recent visit by Brazilian dance group Oba Oba had audiences giving them standing ovations in the middle of the show and raving for days about energy and life affirmation and stuff like that. Dance can, to paraphrase a gridiron commentator I once heard, 'verticalise' your spirits.

And perhaps this new dance group has great things to do or say. Suspender belts on stage will get the audiences in, but I can do without being told it's a fresh idea. Ever heard of *The Rocky Horror Show*? Table-top dancing?

I've got an idea for a heavy-metal modern jazz eisteddfod opera in which that up-himself bloke from *Riverdance* plays Harold Holt with a metaphorical pair of Explorer socks down his Y-fronts. Forty-eight young girlies in see-through negligees will play the public's collective psyche. Grant ahoy, me hearties.

# GHOSTWRITING FOR FERGIE

Recently I was asked by a Sydney newspaper to provide the first paragraph of the Duchess of York's autobiography. But then it seemed difficult to stop. And if Naomi Campbell, the model, can write a novel which she didn't actually write then there would seem no bar to writing even more of the duchess's story, unencumbered by either the facts of the matter or the small impediment of actually not being, in any sense, the Duchess of York.

Every effort will be made to rush it onto the shelves of bookshops and your more classy type of petrol station, to help the cause of the continuing monarchy. Perhaps the duchess will invite me to become her ghost writer. I'm sure she's very busy writing *Budgie the Helicopter* stories and, lately as reported, designing clothes for children.

This designing clothes for children is bound to take up a lot of her time. Drawing wee pairs of trousers, deciding whether French lace Peter Pan collars should be machine washable, test-driving culottes and, of course, choosing the right buckles for the three-year-olds' Swiss skiing outfits—what with also being photographed for *Hello* magazine, *Ta-Ta* magazine and *Feet Fanciers Monthly*, she's going to be pretty stretched.

The autobiography will be called *Is That Another Cream Bun in Your Pocket or Has the Civil List Cheque Just Come Through?* or perhaps *Take My Mother-In-Law—Please!* Here is a brief excerpt:

Even as I mounted the stage to accept the Lady Montague prize for food fighting and fart jokes in the Upper Fourth at St Breeding's, I had little inkling of what was to come. My slightly limpid azure eyes framed by endless girlish lashes gazed out across the rainforest-panelled auditorium, with its plutonium statues of Cupid (eros), Queen Victoria (royalty) and Mandy Rice-Davies (trial by media).

I could see Daddy assisting the Duchess of Haystaque with her anklet and Mamma perusing Debrett's, and yet my only thoughts were to rearrange my uniform skirts, which had become inexplicably tangled about my ears. Oh! My green eyes flashed. How I longed to dash out of doors and fling myself about the grounds coquettishly. So I did.

That's just the sort of girl I was. And I is—carefree, fun-loving, and repellently wealthy. I had not yet learned the art of acrobatic sex with the aristocracy, how to weight my hem with gold ingots so petticoats would not fly up during a helicopter ingress, or even how to sit through a state dinner without flinging the flummeries at Prince Philip. (I defy anybody acquainted with the duke senior not to wish most fervently to fling flummery at almost any juncture, but of course the difference be manners, and I chose the dignified road, keeping flummery flinging to a bare minimum, although I can't say the same of raspberry fool.)

What jolly good fun it was at first, when Andrew and I disported ourselves at Lord Boombah's pheasant-whacking soirees; Andrew so dashing in his bejewelled and bebraided navy jacket and thigh boots and me in calf-length gloves and the Stanislov Tiara. How we laughed

when one of the servants mispronounced Ffolke-
stoneshire, and set the windows a-rattling with our duets
of 'There Was a Young Man from Wig Feenis'.

While Daddy had reminded me at the gymkhana often
enough about the importance of a good seat, I could
hardly be expected to anticipate the impact of my
buttocks on some of the crowned heads of Europe,
through the enterprises of the Fleet Street reporters who
come over so unexpectedly symbiotic, like.

At Sandringham the Royal family proved surprisingly
good at charades and Blind Man's Bluff, but I always felt
for Diana, who according to Fleet Street ought not to be
allowed any buttocks at all. And lack of buttocks be a
definite liability in charades. (And so on.)

# BONKING-CRAZED TOXIC SPIDER ALERT

Richard Ryan's *Funnel Web* is a marvellous book.*
Splendid Australian literature in the rarely-attempted sex-
crazed radioactive giant spider genre.

The Plot: An American nuclear submarine leaks,
causing beachcombing funnel-webs to become nutty. The
spiders get furious at humans for having sex at a party and
one funnel-web runs across the patio, skitter, skitter, and
leaps from ground level to head height and 'pumped every
drop of venom' into a woman identified only as 'silicone-
breasted blonde'.

The spider then behaves somewhat like a European
soccer fan: 'He strutted and postured and posed in grim
celebration. Then, in a hideous reflex, his genitals throbbed
and discharged and he was overcome by an urge to
descend into the earth and copulate.'

Well.

From then on it just gets better and better. There's a
suggestion that spiders are actually from outer space. The
book has maps of the Sydney area which just adds to the
realism as the marauding, bonking-crazed toxic spiders
grow about a metre every few pages and invade the city
killing a fifteen-year-old streetkid on crack in the Cross,
some refugees from Pol Pot, and a lonely old woman.
That's how bad these spidies are.

And then the funnel-webs find a river of poo

* Richard Ryan, *Funnel Web*, Pan Macmillan, 1997.

underneath the city. It's magnificent prose, so let's hear Richard Ryan describe it: 'They gorged on it, their appetites insatiable from the imperative of accelerated growth. And they thrived on it, and grew bigger…and bigger.' Now in case you don't quite get that, a few pages on he reiterates: 'They had nourished themselves on the abundance of fecal matter which flowed to them from every part of the city.'

By this stage the monster spiders are about a metre long, their legs spanning two metres. They rear back and impale people on their fangs which are 'continually dribbling glutinous venom'. A standing height of two to three metres, they move faster than a man could run.

Although he doesn't say whether it's Kim Beazley or Karl Vander-kuyp.

Anyway, by page 104 the funnel-webs have taken over Central Station in Sydney, running into crowds, impaling people and 'gorging on partly liquefied cadavers'. So the army blokes get out there with flamethrowers, but the spiders' venom, atraxotoxin, is now so concentrated that it dissolves skin.

By page 115 a giant girly funnel-web is spinning people into cocoons and hanging them round the walls of the Queen Victoria shopping complex like in *Alien*. Sydney is occupied by giant slavering spiders.

So a former RAAF hero decides to bomb the Warragamba Dam and flood the joint because spiders don't like water. Again, the realism is tremendous. We know the hero flew Lincolns in Malaya, 'a variant of the Avro Lancaster as flown by the RAF themselves in the latter part of the war'. (In 1971 he was flying a Republic F-105 Thunderchief in Cambodia.) Anyway, it doesn't work. The spiders are still on the rampage.

The politicians decide to drop a radiation bomb which only makes the spiders worse, but not before they are 'vomiting uncontrollably and the contents of their intestines pouring out of them in jets of bloody excrement'. Then they start eating each other. The new generation of funnel-webs are 'much more massively powerful with eight legs like tree trunks', and spanning eight or nine metres. These ones go around ripping off roofs and chasing refugees up and down mountains, impaling and eating them and then 'frolicked in the remains of their ill-fated victims'.

In the end they take over the whole eastern side of Australia except Tassie. Western Australia secedes and is invaded by Indonesia, a crabby funnel-web sprays acid venom all over the Sydney Harbour Bridge, which collapses, the old PM has the New South Wales premier's plane shot down, the new Australian PM is a CIA agent, the ten-metre-tall spiders rule Australia.

But my favourite scene in the book is when they nuke the Brindabella Ranges with US missiles, like backburning. And what happens? The funnel-webs just dance into the trough. Hundreds of them out in the bush waving their fangs around and getting down. Dead funky. Crap book but.

# THE GENESIS OF
## *THE LITTLE BOOK OF STRESS*

Further investigations are continuing into the self-help market. You may find this hard to believe, but there is yet another one of those weeny books with one sentence on each page which will totally revolutionise your life to the point where you will look in the mirror and see a stranger—and have conniptions. (Whatever conniptions are, probably some kind of kitten.)

Anyway, this book, which is just big enough to momentarily stun a cockroach, is called *The Little Book of Calm* by Paul Wilson and features TWO drawings of a cloud and ONE thought per page (which, let's face it, is about as much as you want from any book. If you want more than one thought a page, try *Moby Dick* or the ABC charter or something.)

On the back of the new weeny book it says, 'Open it at any page and you will find a path to inner peace'. I opened the book and it said, 'WEAR WHITE. The clothes you wear have a distinct influence on the way you feel. Loose garments, natural fabrics and light colours all lead to calm. This is why yogis wear white.'

One might venture to suggest that yogis wear white because they don't have to wash their own clothes. And also because yogis walk around the joint being a bit spiritual most of the time and never have to strip a carburettor, or pick up a two-year-old who has been rolling in banana, sand, spit and tanbark in that order. If anybody who isn't a yogi wears white, after about five minutes they look like they've been mud-wrestling a distressed eel. And come second.

Mr Wilson also suggests that if one removes one's wristwatch, one is removed from time and pressures. (This thought made me so stressed I strapped a penguin to my head and went to taunt polar bears at the zoo.) If you remove your watch and then miss all the appointments you need to keep a job and a social life, you might instead be rather swiftly removed from income and friends.

Mr Wilson further advises that, 'By moving slowly, speaking calmly, you can spread a feeling of calm within a group.' Unless they think you're on heroin and call the dog squad, which would probably put the mockers on the calm concept. Other suggestions include 'massage your eyebrows', 'be up for the sunrise' (Good Lord, surely a misprint) and to watch fish. (I stared at a haddock fillet for three hours and felt nothing but a strange sense of foreboding and morbid dread.) He also recommends singing Christmas songs. The man obviously has never been trapped in a shopping-mall elevator featuring the muzak tape of 'Jingle Bells'. And who amongst us can get to the chorus of 'Frosty the Snowman' without suddenly feeling violent?

If people follow Mr Wilson's advice we'll be nothing but a country of wafty, passive hippies dressed like a tennis party. Dreadful policies will be announced by the government and we'll all just pop off for a lie-down on a patchouli-scented futon, having sex (just for the calm moments afterwards) and looking longingly at anchovies when the credit-card bills arrive.

Consequently, what the world needs is *The Little Book of Stress*. Readers are invited to contribute their own suggestions, but I think we can make a good start with: 'Begin the day with three long blacks, a coke and a packet of Peter Stuyvesant', 'Watch the news', 'Why not plan a holiday in a war zone?', 'Have sex with all the married people in your workplace' and 'Give birth to as many children as you can one after the other and then take up with a temperamental rock star'.

After *The Little Book of Stress* takes the publishing world by storm, we'll continue to redress the balance with *The Bumper Book of Hideous Thoughts*, *The Paranoia Book for Boys*, *The Girls' Own Annual of Antsiness* and *Panic Attacks for Beginners*. In the meantime, just take a few minutes each day to brood about any imagined insults and eat a lot of red food-colouring, paint your bedroom orange and stand on traffic islands shouting at random vehicles. Some of us have to keep an edge.

# THE FESTIVAL OF BANGING ON

Just back from a writers' festival. It's a *tremendous* idea, the festival of the writer. What happens is, somebody pays for you to fly to another city and puts you up in a flash hotel for a few days and you don't have to wash your own towels, and all you have to do is pop out every now and again and crap on about books or ideas or something. And then the audience asks you questions.

Such as 'Where do you get your ideas from?' (A bloke called Ern at The Abbotsford front bar) 'How do you get published?' (Suck up to publishers) and 'What's the time? I don't want to miss the start of Princess Diana's funeral.' (No answer as writer desperately ferrets through cerebral built-in-robes for a cloak of witty comeback and comes up starkers.)

Some writers piked out of their scheduled readings so they could watch the funeral but some went ahead, not least those of us under the command of an immensely amusing Ms Mary Rose McColl, a Brisbane writer who hosted a women writers' event called All Frocked Up in a frock (nay, gown) of such flounciness, such furbelowing, such utter pinkness, such incredible-off-the-shoulderity that one gasped with envy. Minx.

Usually there are all sorts of fondling frenzies at a writers' festival as author groupies try to score with whoever (or whomever—must ask a writer) becomes the Incoming Star of the Festival. The carpets of flash hotels get little paths worn from the lifts to the Famous Offshore

Writer's Boudoir. But somebody had been sensible at the Brisbane Writers' Festival. There were no legions of lone, one-book-wonder poncy poets of Russian/Cockney/Belgian heritage with Basset Hound eyes going, 'I, am a famous Writah. 'Ere, 'oo wants a root?' types. (There was a writer's husband who had failed to grasp the mood, who kept popping up next to her like a roller blind saying 'HELLO! I'm her HUSBAND!' and startling people out of their wits.)

And, natch, here were the usual writahs who, allocated ten minutes in a panel session, bunged it on and would BANG ON for more than half an hour and had to be bludgeoned off the podium.

And there was an amazing performance by Bryce Courtenay, who sells squillions of books (good on him) and is trying to get a splendid-sounding scheme off the ground to have old people read to little kids and help them learn at school.

The audience was spellbound as he told a story about how when he finished the manuscript of *The Power of One* (estimated Australasian sales: 789 kerjillion) he wrapped it up and used it as a doorstop in the kitchen for a year and then somebody literally tripped over it and reminded him it was there and so it was sent to a publisher and the rest is…you know.

By jingo, I thought. That bloke should try writing fiction. He's a berloody natural.

# THE FESTIVAL OF FAFFING FERALS

I knew it was going to be a strange day when I woke up on Sunday morning and there was a giant inflatable Toohey's Blue can at the end of my street.

Yes, it was the fringe festival of Fitzroy otherwise known as the Festival of Faffing Ferals. It seemed that every person in the world with dreadlocks who lives in the Southern Hemisphere got up yesterday, had fourteen bucket bongs and popped down to my street.

I've had time to make a bit of an anthropological study of ferals and this is what I've come up with:

Favourite mode of transport: sitting down on the footpath.

Favourite outfit: pants, dress, skirt, jacket on backwards, small knitted hot-water-bottle-cover on head, optional face paint and full-body piercing. It's probably easier to say which bits are not pierced on a feral and so far I've been able to identify the knees, elbows and buttocks—but most of this is hearsay evidence.

Favourite hobbies: crap busking: didgeridoo playing, clapsticks, any kind of percussion pinched from an indigenous group that you can use to beg money with. This is surprisingly effective. Yesterday I gave a Swedish Rastafarian-looking gentleman $2.50 because he promised to stop playing the didgeridoo. The wild earthly fusion of techno, percussion and tinkly new-age bells creates a new melange music for the nineties: This is what Brunswick Street sounded like yesterday.

Street theatre is a bit of a forte, though I'm not sure that the feral safety officers will be pleased at the news that a fire-eating person ended up with serious burns at the festival.

Being feral is a beautiful expression of individualism and especially good because you all get to have the same haircut.

And if you've lost anything at all, a pair of thongs, the car keys, a couple of aircraft carriers—just check your nearest feral—there nestling among the dreadlocks will be a few lost travel-allowance forms, two banana lounges and the odd aircraft carrier feared lost in the Bermuda Triangle.

# A Degree of Disagree

When William Dobell's portrait of fellow artist Joshua Smith won the Archibald Prize in 1943, a couple of narked also-rans in the Archie arc-ed up, claiming it was a caricature, and asked the Supreme Court to say the prize shouldn't have been awarded. (Joshua Smith himself, whose entry ran second, was not among them.) The judge decided it was a portrait.

Not long ago in Melbourne there was a debate on the question, more than fifty years later, to raise funds for a gallery: arty feuds in this country seem to go forever. And the need for everything to be presented as a conflict (or 'debate') seems as unquenchable as the chimera.

A high-ranking former Cabinet minister was recently trying to rustle up some 'talent', as they say in network telly, to debate the proposition (if memory serves) that 'Australian Men Are a Pack of Useless No-hoper Idiots'. Some felt forced graciously to decline on the grounds of domestic harmony and getting the garbage put out in the usual way.

Analysis as a gladiatorial team sport is all the go. Before elections they always have 'head to heads', redolent of nothing so much as moose-rutting season. If you want ratings all you have to do is put into a TV studio the following: Pauline Hanson, Bruce Ruxton, Graeme Campbell, anybody called Beryl or Stan, some students with nose rings and a bag of angel dust and/or Richard Carleton. Stir, and you're away. Easy peasy.

There have been offers to debate the point of romance, whether most Australian novels are crap, and who pinched most of the doona (okay, that was at home). Debating the niceties of whether an old painting was a portrait or not seemed a lot safer.

Some of the best paintings in the last few Archies have been by painter and Australian caricaturist Bill Leak. Not that his paintings look like cartoons. But I suspect he sees things differently, perhaps a little sharper, and that is part of his, well, art.

When Justice Roper decided in 1943 that William Dobell's painting was allowed to retain the Archibald Prize, he found that a portrait should display a sense of likeness, and that including the face in a portrait was 'perhaps essential'. On the evidence, you'd have to disagree with the learned bloke in the wig.

A while ago, cartoonist Michael Leunig depicted our excruciating prime minister returning from his overseas visit during which, as a man of the future, he had visited a deserted cricket ground, a Baroness Thatcher and a Mister Newt Gingrich.

The thing about the Leunig portrait is that it did not show the prime minister's face. Indeed, there was no need to. Howard was instantly recognisable. Who else could it be, a tiny man with nothing to declare at customs, certainly no genius, the most dis-Wildean figure in living history.

Art can be anything. A performance artist could give you a bite of a horrid, floury green banana, saying: 'That taste is a portrait of the Labor Party's policy on youth employment.' Fair enough. I may be telegraphing my debating punches here, but I reckon if somebody does something and calls it a portrait, then it's a portrait. I can't be bothered arguing about it. No wonder 'Sixty Minutes' never calls.

# 6
# Politicklish

# PHWOOOAAAARRRRR

Is there any particular reason why so many cartoonists and journalists get so utterly FREAKED by the idea of (titter) a woman (phwoaaarrrrrr) joining a new political party (way-heyyyyyy) that every original idea flies out of their heads (like that scene in *Alien* when Ripley opens the side bay and the alien gets sucked out into space) and they have to draw pictures of Cheryl Kernot as Juliet, a bosom-baring Boadicea (I think you'll find most women leaders of history are uncontrollable exhibitionists) or a flushed, floppy, sated, naked chick under the sheets who's just been thoroughly rogered by Kim Beazley AND Gareth Evans (as if), or she's described as 'seduced', 'wedded', 'married', 'wooed' and, one imagines but for the sharp eyes of a roving sub-editor, 'THOROUGHLY ROGERED', and... 'shivering as his political manhood hardened. She ran a perfectly manicured finger dipped in chocolate crackles down the front of his briefing papers'?

That was rather a long sentence. Unfortunately the subs are too busy putting their pencil through Kernot stories with the word 'love pump' in them.

I know it's a challenge to get up a political cartoon at short notice, but some people manage to find an image that doesn't look like a sanitised catalogue for mysterious bakelite marital aids with hand-whiffling attachments. And hello, how come the girrrl politician is always the passive, dopey one in these scenarios?

The commentators are so fixated on the idea that the

former Democrats leader was a passive wallflower who moped around until she got 'seduced' they've missed the obvious 'Wanton Kernot Has Her Way with ALP: Short Foreplay' or 'Shameless Hussy Puts the Moves On' possibilities. Not to mention: 'Kernot Grabs a Short-cut to Prime Minister. Crean to Get Stuffed.'

I mean, when Mal Colston ran away from home clutching nothing but an old oxygen mask which had dropped from the ceiling in the event of an emergency, did we get cartoons of Kim Beazley sobbing with a broken heart? Or calling 11-505-RAUNCHY to fill his aching need? Was Robert Ray depicted as the crazed stalker, driven mad by a love which turned to a twisted obsession?

Were we subjected to cartoons of John Howard offering Mal bunches of flowers and a quickie on the frontbench? Did we get headlines about nuptials and rooting and carry-on up the sheltershed shenanigans? Were there hilarious little drawings of Peter Reith with his hands down Mr Colston's Y-fronts? Was Mr Colston depicted as the great nude army deserter of history?

When the prime minister was promising Senator Harradine an end to contraception for anybody over the age of nought, or whatever the deal was, to get him to vote for flogging off Telstra, did editorialists have Howard wearing leather chaps in a gay bar chatting up the snowy-haired senator in a sleeveless T-shirt and hiking boots? And when the deal was done, were there any images of the two of them in the cot after a vigorous shagging, sharing a cigar and port?

Not bloody likely. That'd be offensive.

# WORLD LEADER SHIRT FIASCO

With rumours now running around like a crazed ferret that the next APEC meeting is to be held in Dubbo, the Department of Foreign Affairs has turned its attention away from sucking up to Indonesia to consider the problem of World Leader Shirting.

This is not to be confused with Shirty World Leaders, another feature of economic meetings, it is instead the emerging tradition of the world leaders frocking up for the conference. Last year in Jakarta (don't mention the war) all the boys wore batik long-sleeved numbers of varying designs. This week, they all slithered into Filipino peasant blousery and waved at the camera like a delegation of somewhat demented dentists trying to halt the traffic.

Lucky they're all blokes, our eighteen APEC World Leaders, or there might have been some serious mumu-type involvement. Anyway, with this charming convention set to continue, the Dubbo APEC Fancy Dress and Funding Committee has come up with some fabulous suggestions, apart from a Portuguese lamington drive.

World Leaders will be clobbered in traditional Australian costume, consisting primarily of a faded navy blue singlet, a pair of shorts pulled down to reveal a fifty-cent bum crack, and a sturdy pair of wackeda-wackeda rubber thonging devices, for the feet. Each World Leader will be supplied with an APEC Souvenir Stubby Holder and a pair of serviceable barbecue tongs. All will be coached in the time-honoured shouting of the Australian greeting, 'Get us another beer, would you darl?'

In the unlikely event of any female World Leader fronting on the day, Mrs Lorraine Thud has agreed to run up a couple of crimplene suits on her Singer Turbo. Mrs Heather Cack will be on stand-by with cardies in case of inclemency on a large scale.

World-renowned Australian folk singers including the Thompson Twins, Kev and Thommo, will welcome the leaders with some dinky-di Aussie songs including 'God Save the Queen', 'When Irish Eyes Are Smiling', 'The Locomotion' and the convict favourite, 'Hey Now, My Boyfriend's Back'.

An All Australian Food festival will kick off the first night's entertainment, including Yorkshire Pudding, Worcestershire sauce and Cornish pasties, to be washed down with Earl Grey tea and Fat Bagpipe custard.

Cultural workshops will be conducted by the Member for Manners, and Oxley, a woman whose name escapes me but almost rhymes with Fraulein Pantson. Mrs Pantson has been doing terrific work this week being rude to Aboriginal people. It certainly takes the lamington to complain that there's nothing disadvantaged about Aboriginal people in the week that a report shows that the Aboriginal deaths-in-custody rate is now worse than before we held a Royal Commission into the tragic high rates of same.

On this point, that there is nothing special about the current needs of Aboriginal people, Mrs Pantson is difficult to argue with. (Partly because she keeps walking out or not turning up. Partly because she seems to have no knowledge of statistics in the areas of infant mortality, health services, death rates, disease rates, the availability of fresh water, sewerage, housing, employment, historical and continuing discrimination, arrest rates for minor offences, ignorance and flouting of the recommendations of the aforementioned Royal Commission, cervical cancer rates, hearing loss, blindness, the placement of nuclear bomb tests in living memory, and the like.)

Of course, it could be that 'freedom of speech' also gives some people the ability to tell one-size-fits-all porkies, even porkies that they believe in despite the evidence. Perhaps we could put it in a nicer way and borrow a phrase from one of Florence Nightingale's less hagiographic biographers, who described her as a 'titil-lating fabulist'.

Consequently, Mrs Pantson will be running workshops for the World Leaders on: 'Titillating Fabulism: Its Place in Media Briefings'; 'Posing for Publicity Photographs with a Plate of Fish and Chips'; 'Zenophobia: Fear of Zens'; and 'Purse-Lipped Whingeing: An Australian Cultural History for Beginners'. Tickets on herself at the door.

# INFILTRATION SITUATION

The Melbourne papers were recently chockers with how the police were 'so successful' at infiltrating conservation groups that they 'helped staff their offices, produced newsletters and updated membership lists'. Hang on. How about: 'Conservation groups got so much free work out of the police in Melbourne they didn't need to hire office staff for years'?

Several years ago, on police pay, an officer wrote an entire Aboriginal land rights policy and another spent two days building shelves for Friends of the Earth. One brought cake to Wilderness Society meetings. A few produced a left-wing community radio station breakfast show. Two cops lectured on the dangers of extreme nationalism for a group called Radical Women. This is obviously some sort of tremendous scheme where cops support left-wing groups at our expense.

Other officers spent our money taking photos of customers at bookshops selling books on the environment (how suspicious is THAT) and staking out Evonne's Cafe in Apollo Bay because Evonne had failed to express a whole-hearted passion for the practice of woodchipping.

Police were getting out there—maybe they still are—without the government even knowing, bugging phones, searching without a warrant and frocking up as feminists. Eh? Yes, cop this headline from last Tuesday: 'Female Police Posed as Feminists'.

What went on at *that* briefing? 'Ladies. I'm Detective

Senior Sergeant Wheatbag, in charge of the new squad of fake feminists. Get us a coffee would you, love? While you're down there—only jokin'.

'Anyway, you'll be infiltrating weirdy femmo groups, a dangerous bunch who want better kindergarten facilities, less violence, and to have meetings which involve the code phrase, "Bring a Plate". Find out what that's all about. Secondly, you'll need to look the part. Brian?'

'Yeah, thanks Wheaty. Girls, your kit: New Integrated Feminist. Bouffant wig, chin bow, slide rule, overalls and stiletto heels. Or, Kit Two: Lipstick Lezzo. Doc Marten lace-ups, lurex boob tube, plastic rain bonnet, blokey strides and an eyebrow pencil with a poison dart in it.

'Right. You lot penetrating Friends of the Earth. They're hard to pin down, so Robbo, tea-cosy on your noggin and sing Enya all the time. Clarice'll need a three-piece for lobbying Canberra. Anyone got a degree in biology? No? Bugger.

'And for God's sake, you sheilas, stay in character. Remember what happened to Constable Clanger at the Wilderness Society? Spent six months in a mangy koala suit and blew his cover when his mo got stuck in the zipper and he used the c word. And, hey. Be careful out there.'

According to leaked files, cops spied on gay groups (playing Kylie Minogue records backwards for hidden messages, maybe) and the Council for Civil Liberties, whatever that is.

Anyway, the cops were also watching Women in Black, a small group disbanded in 1993 when their goal materialised: Israeli-Palestinian peace talks. They held weekly vigils at the Melbourne GPO, dressed in black, all six to twenty of them. Imagine the agony of the poor under-cover cop trying to gather information. At a silent vigil. On a Saturday morning. In a little black dress.

A former member remembers a few would-be members from that time were rejected: 'Nutters, or anti-Semitic, so they got quickly dumped off.' Now, you've got to wonder whether some of the 'nutters' were the police, testing the waters.

'Well, sir, I then moved to the left-hand side of what I now know to be the lounge room, waved a picture of Mel Brooks, shouted "Death to the Shah!" and then, "Ha ha ha! Anyone for molotov cocktails?!" Sir, I never saw them again, sir.'

Former Women in Black members recall that people would come to the vigils and take photos, presumably to check whether Yasser Arafat was there in a wraparound skirt. One said this week she was thrilled anybody had taken any notice.

All the groups 'infiltrated' sounded flattered, confused, or couldn't stop laughing long enough to talk. One bloke from the Friends of the Earth reckoned the land rights policy was never used and the well-meaning copper put the shelves up at the wrong height. 'We're thinking of sending the police a bill next week, for replacing them,' he said.

Even more amused was the Melbourne branch of the international socialist group Radical Women, a small band who police claim had a cunning plan—look out—to block Hoyts cinema loos. 'We were on the picket line with Hoyts workers,' said a spokeswoman. 'We're trade unionists ourselves. But to get into blocking *toilets*? It's bizarre.'

Never mind the personal privacy issues and the fact that cops never seem to infiltrate weird right-wing groups like the BHP board and, oh, I don't know, the federal Cabinet, the H. R. Nicholls Lamington Fanciers of Shepparton and the Hugh Morgan Fan Club.

The real point is what if the undercover cops have turned? What if community double-agents have infiltrated the force, intent on encouraging respect for democratic grassroots political action and teaching constables how to bring a plate? You can't be too careful.

# SCHOOL'S OUT—WAY OUT

Mindful of the prime minister's desire to see our little kiddiewinks taught less about our racist past and more about, oh, the history of cheese-whacking in the Hunter District, we here at History R Us have devised the bare bones of a new Australian curriculum.

## THINGS TO BE PROUD OF

Gallipoli (the thing to be proud of about Gallipoli is that the young men sent to Turkey in order to be killed were brave and innovative. Not that they were sent by bouff-brained 'superiors' with all the military strategy of a mad possum in a bag). Also, mateship (the thing to be proud of here is that men loved each other and looked after each other in a silent, manly sort of way. For example, to indicate physical affection, one could club one's mate over the head with a mattock or fence post. Better to overlook the idea of mateship as applied in the past to women and people who were slightly not sort of Caucasian). Wheat production, the introduction of the ugg boot to California as a fashion item, and Mel Gibson (born in England).

## THINGS NOT TO BE PROUD OF

Nil. Children must be taught to be personally proud of the good things in Australia's past and to feel totally unconnected to any bad things in the past, especially if it's easier to pretend the bad things did not happen at all. It's always better to sweep a huge pile of steaming wombat droppings under the carpet in the living room. Nobody will notice, if they know what's good for them.

## THE WHITE AUSTRALIA POLICY
Never happened. This is a misprint for the Australian Whitegoods Policy, instituted by Sir Eyebrows Menzies in a speech in 1066 at Hastings. (Or Pambula, maybe.) Anyway, by means of this policy, all Australians were allowed to import one government-subsidised fridge, washing machine, blowfly-zapper or microwave oven (invented by a Mrs McFarlane Burnett on the goldfields) for personal use.

## ABORIGINAL MASSACRES
This, of course, refers to the scores in early football matches when Aboriginal teams tended to slaughter their opposition, a bunch of English private school imports with handstitched leather boots, cravats, riding jackets and parachute-silk shorts. For example, here is the originally recorded score for a match in approximately 1689, which was called off due to bad light and a spot of black plague. Us, hurrah, hurrah: 0. Tinted Fellows in the Nuddy: 3,453,637 goals, 3 points. Shortly thereafter all the Aboriginal people known to the authorities went on a cruise near the Bermuda Triangle and disappeared.

## THE STOLEN GENERATIONS
We shall stop teaching that thousands of Aboriginal children were ripped from their sobbing mothers, or stolen while their mothers were down the shops. Because for one thing, many of those children were better off, according

to some government figures, because they were given a slap-up education. Not perhaps, in areas such as Latin grammar and who their parents were, but by jingo some of those dark lasses could get a collar stain out with a couple of hours of elbow grease and a bit of old Velvet soap. Those girls got to know about hospital corners on sheets, polishing silver and getting the master's boots jolly shiny.

And anybody questioning why Aboriginal kids were given a better education after being taken away from their parents is a troublemaking unpatriotic pleb. There is no point setting up decent schools in the bush. Can't remember why, but it's in a report from the Protectorate of Public Funds, 1945, paragraph 56 sub-paragraph 67 sub-woofer 45.

## THE FUTURE

Those children who have been calling other kids nigger and slope mongrel in the playground will be asked nicely to keep the noise down during any visits from our vastly respected trading partners. Other than that, it's free speech ahoy.

## OTHER SUBJECTS

We are expanding into new areas of curriculum shortly, with Geography R Us (Tasmania who? East Timor is north of Java!), Maths R Us (six times seven is 93 and a half!) and Science R Them (Dinosaurs, Shminosaurs).

# GERN LAWS

As a law-abiding citizen without a criminal record involving violence (that sounds more tantalising than it is, a bit like the movie *Showgirls* of which more later) I don't see why I can't be allowed to own a rocket launcher, some anti-personnel mines and an aircraft carrier. (I'm going to use them to kill rabbits, which is a bugger of a problem in the suburbs. There are bunnies busting out all over and begging to be blown away. Some of the bastards are in hutches but I've got an engineer working on the problem.)

One of the things the Gern Larby wants is crimping. And I have to say to them, 'No you don't.' Have they no sense of history, for God's sake? Can't they remember that crimping done to Olivia Newton-John at about the time of her mauve leotard period? And was it reversible? Was it ever. Soon after it was the Farrah Fawcett Cut, the Sharpie Cut and then The One Where Just the Fringey Bits Were Flicked Back, and then, one thing led to another, people moved onto the hard stuff—the Shag Look. (Which was, at least, rather more sophisticated that the Utterly Shagged Look.)

Crimping is the worst hairstyle since the Dolly cut—a seventies pterodactyl of a high-maintenance do that went with light-blue eyeshadow and involved either putting your wet hair into 17,000 plaits until it dried, or using a 'crimper', a device not unlike a waffle iron but which would singe hair into that crinkle-cut look so beloved, it seems, by Ted Drane, national president of the Sporting Shooters' Association. (Unsporting shooters have been unavailable for comment, unless you believe actions speak louder than words.) Face it, Ted, better to go for a good quality bouffant wiglet.

So, it's obviously time for a referendum. Otherwise, premiers and chief ministers will change their minds before their next election and the whole thing will be cactus. Apparently we are a democracy, which means if the majority of people in a majority of states want something we get it (unless you count a holiday house and some gold ingots). It only remains to frame the questions. Referendums are very expensive, so they always try to cram as many questions on at once. At the last referendum I was a remote polling officer in the Northern Territory, being flown around Uluru and its surrounds in a wee plane by a pilot called Angus McSporran (this is perfectly true).

As I recall, there were four IMPORTANT QUESTIONS for the future of the country: should we have people on juries? What's the capital of Argentina? How do you make a dry martini? Who is going to win the Grand Final? No, no, maybe they were: should you wear socks with sandals? what is the chemical symbol for Neptunium? and…ahem. I've just called Excellent Steve at the Electoral Commission who says the questions were basically do you want the constitution altered to provide: four-year parliamentary terms, fair and democratic elections throughout Australia, local government recognised and a triple bunger—an extension of the right to trial by jury, freedom of religion and fair terms for any property compulsorily acquired by the government? The country voted 'No, shut up, don't understand' to all of these.

(Imagine explaining to an elderly Aboriginal lady hounded off her own home to make way for some cows and violently relieved of her children by the state that she is voting on fair terms for any 'property' compulsorily acquired.)

Anyway, this time, the questions must be clear:

1. Should anyone with a gun that shoots heaps of bullets turn it over to police to avoid accidents, unforeseen madness and a fearful ambience?

2. Should the Gern Larby just bugger off to Montana, America?

3. Should former *Twin Peaks* Agent Cooper, Kyle McLachlan, give up hoping ever to get a job again after being in *Showgirls*, winner of Crap Movie of the Decade, and is that a false chin, or what?

4. Do you want a cup of tea? Or for brevity's sake: Should the federal government have full control of gun laws and should Ted Drane go the bouffant?

# ULTIMATE EXECUTIVE ACTION FIGURES

Now that the Tempe High languages school in Sydney's west has decided to deploy armed security guards to patrol the grounds and guard the gates, a whole new world of job opportunities has opened up, and there's no shortage of the unemployed to fill them.

Yes, the education department need only lift the phone and call Sandline International. 'I hear you've just had forty mercenaries deported from Papua New Guinea. I'm in a position to offer them immediate redeployment on tuckshop duty starting at 0700 hours Monday.'

The mercenaries were to have amused themselves by training the PNG army to deal with the rebel forces on Bougainville Island, home to the inoperative Panguna copper mine and about 180,000 items of potential collateral damage (people).

The PNG army weren't all that thrilled about the idea of the mercenaries mainly because they were to be paid about $46 million and the PNG soldiers haven't been getting decent shoes or, for example, lunch. So they've kicked them out.

Obviously there will be others clamouring for the services of the trained killers that English company Sandline hired from a company called Executive Outcomes, a named which conjures up the image of 300 businessmen in double-breasted suits, packing a cut lunch in their briefcase and a couple of grenade launchers each.

The Albanians will be putting in a bid for help with a

couple of diversions such as fleeing the country, looting King Zog's palace and placing armed boys on the street at a time of their life we can only refer to as the Festival of Testosterone. The Albanian bid will be hampered by the fact that their Gross National Product adds up to about $2.50 on a good day.

The Executive Outcomes lads do not come cheap, and sure, the government might have to cut a few school libraries and special elective education programs, such as maths. But it's a small price to pay for the polished role models the mercenaries could present.

Already the people who will be walking around schoolyards with guns have cottoned onto the idea of naming your company something splendidly neutral: Ultimate Security. Accordingly, it is believed guards will be carrying handguns, dummies, and a fluffy pinstriped bunny rug similar to the one Linus carries around in the *Peanuts* comic strip. This will be referred to as the Ultimate Executive Security Blanket.

This is not quite the image required, and when the boys from Executive Outcomes arrive with their Russian helicopter gunships and camouflage gear, the standard will be raised. Tuckshops will be issued with cattle prods and defensive razor wire, and the parents' committee will be required to wear balaclavas and meet in portable class-rooms renamed Ultimate Bunkers.

Target practice for kids who have attached themselves to the guards as work-experience students will be held on the oval every alternating Thursday, and hand-to-hand combat will be co-ordinated by Mrs Alistair 'Gumpy'

Pritchett, formerly head of drama and director of the acclaimed nativity play division of HQ. Girls' stiletto classes, formerly something to do with shoes, will now be conducted under the supervision of Miss Miranda Fortesque, formerly of St Trinian's.

Sandline will provide some of the equipment, for example, exploding bullets and cigars. Strenuous measures will be taken to avoid a repeat of the Angola–Sierra Leone situation when the Sandline steamer trunks were opened at a government cocktail party, only to reveal normal bullets and exploding cigars. Dispatch has been dealt with and relatives request that donations be made to the Artificial Limbs Repatriation Centre. No flowers.

Naturally, the men from Executive Outcomes will not be involved in the conflicts themselves, but will assume an advisory role, providing training such as, 'Go for the eye-gouge first and THEN the bayoneting, Jason', and 'What did I say was the first rule of flamethrowers, Mandy? That's right, go for the torso, not the ponytail. This is not a scrag-fight, Mandy, it's war.'

# TIME TO SPRAY

It's been a weirdy week, hasn't it? David Jones sees its share price dip and blames it on women not buying enough fashion. Well, would you if the choice was between a lime green polyester shirt that makes you look like a wombat in a wheat bag or a $10,000 pure white wool suit with pant legs longer than your entire body?

And also, the nation was ruled by the deputy prime minister, Tim Fischer, for the entire week. I don't know whether you would have heard of him. He's the SECOND most powerful bloke in the country because his National Party—including Country Liberal Party candidates—got a smidge more than EIGHT per cent of the first preference vote at the last election (it's democracy, darling).

Mr Fischer has all the charisma, sharp wit and general appearance of a gingerbread man, except that he always wears a bush hat, even in capital cities. It is not clear whether he does this because he thinks it will make him look more effectively rural, or because he is a dickhead. Mr Fischer's many pronouncements on foreign affairs and other matters have produced little more than astonished smirking, once translated from a kind of revved-up Joh-speak.

Mr Fischer's demeanour is best explained by imagining a large, hairy, wet labrador. At first, he seems harmless and lovable but soon displays not the slightest grasp of any situation, knocking over the beer and weeing on the carpet.

At the risk of overworking the canine theme, let us not forget the much-flogged adage about lying down with dogs and getting up with fleas. Mr Fischer leads the National Party branch members who dribble so enthusiastically at Pauline Hanson's endless whining, and also Bob Katter jnr, member for somewhere screamingly rednecked in Queensland, who snipes about Aborigines and 'poofs'.

It is not known why Mr Katter is so interested in banging on about poofs, or why he is interested in other people's sex lives. Mr Katter looks to have the florid, repressed, imminently explosive look of a man who doesn't get enough of it. Publicity, I mean. The man needs a damn good rooting around. In his psyche.

Mr Fischer, who is charged with the responsibility of representing people in remote areas, seems to think this means white people in remote areas. He said in 1994 that it would be a waste of money providing tap water to some Aboriginal communities (a basic human right, we're not talking about a travertine marble daiquiri fountain) because Aboriginal children would not know how to use the taps or would vandalise the equipment.

More recently, after being led around chosen bits of Tibet by a Chinese delegation, Mr Fischer said he thought the Chinese invasion was going swimmingly for Tibetans.

As it is every Christmas break, the media, with Mr Fischer's help, showed him as a mildly nice guy who's in charge while the PM's on holidays. The danger is to see only the loping, dimwitted, harmlessly amusing side of the labrador and forget that they are usually represented very high up on the list of dog breeds which savage small children. It is the National Party members which generally believe that women should just pop off out the back and make themselves useful with a spare spatula or uterus.

Many National Party members like the idea of getting around in long socks and semiautomatic weapons (although to be fair many of this lot now see the National Party as too left-wing for them and are a bit keen on the One Nation lot. Eek).

National and Country Liberal Party politicians get out in front, wave their jowls and their comparatively weeny vote and lobby hard against the *Mabo* and *Wik* decisions because they can't bring themselves to consider the idea of negotiating with Aborigines on an equal footing, or in many cases of acknowledging that Aborigines have legal rights which might predate their own.

If Tim Fischer seems like a bad joke now, wait for the punchline.

LATER: After these remarks went to press, I had a telephone call from a deputy editor of a major Australian newspaper in which they were published, who was very upset that they *had* been published. 'Tim,' he told me, 'is upset.' If I wanted to write any more on the subject of politics, I was to submit it all to the deputy editor. Not, he hastened to add, for the purposes of political censorship, but on the matter of taste. I should not have called the deputy prime minister a dickhead because 'he was a nice guy' and furthermore, 'He won't stand in the way of the *Wik* decision—he's not like that.' For the record, a week later Mr Fischer went feral about *Wik*, eventually ensuring white leaseholders of pastoral lands they would get 'bucketfuls of extinguishment'.

# THE SHUT RIGHT UP CAMPAIGN

When little kids don't want to hear something, they scowl, stick their fingers in their ears and sing really loudly, 'La la laaa!' Or in some cases, 'Nerny, nerny ner.'

Remind you of anyone?

The Coalition government, faced with so much upset and opposition to its proposed amendments to the Native Title Act, just tells everyone else to SHUT RIGHT UP.

The churches, to a denomination, came out against the prime minister's so-called *Wik* 10-Point Plan of amendments. The prime minister told the lot of them to SHUT UP—you don't, he said snippily, have a monopoly on morals.

Senator Herron, who is apparently the Minister for Aboriginal Affairs but not so you'd notice, says the churches who oppose the plan are ill-informed. People should SHUT UP unless they read the entire legislation and explain each paragraph. One is tempted to tell Mr Herron that if that is the case, he should have sent a copy of the legislation, the amendments and the government's intent, to every house in the country before putting it to parliament. If one could find him.

The central intention of the amendments is to destroy or 'extinguish' rights that Aboriginal native title holders have over land that is leased by a pastoralist. Aborigines with a family ownership of land stretching back thousands of years will have no access or restricted access to land which is owned by the Australian people and leased to pastoralists—including Kerry Packer, federal Cabinet minister Ian McLachlan and oh, fancy, the north Queensland backbencher Warren Entsch, who last week told country people to boycott their churches because they hadn't SHUT UP.

In many places, the 'co-existence' of pastoralists and Aborigines on leasehold property is just worked out by agreement among themselves.

The 'certainty' that the plan will give pastoralists on 'their' land means they can suddenly start commercial operations such as logging. For many this will be a great financial advantage over ordinary farmers who paid outright for freehold land, which is unaffected by native title. (Mr Entsch says he won't be making a windfall profit, he'll only get the certainty. That's all right then. Good job he chairs the coalition's Native Title committee.)

Mr Entsch claims the church leaders 'have not been speaking to people in the rural areas', denied by clerics such as the Anglican Archbishop in Perth. Mr Entsch seems to imply that only non-Aboriginal pastoralists who support the plan live outside the cities, a rather odd concept for somebody who is supposed to represent Cape York and the Torres Strait Islands in Parliament.

Another bloke who had a go at the churches claiming they were 'ill-informed' (i.e. SHUT UP you haven't read the legislation backwards in Swahili) was former Senator Noel Crichton-Browne, from Perth (you'll recall he's the one who greeted a female journalist with 'I'll screw your tits off') who said church opposition to the plan was a contributing factor to declining church membership.

The Archbish quietly pointed out that pew-fillers were up 8 to 10 per cent in the major cities.

One of the line-dancers in the SHUT RIGHT UP campaign is the president of the Western Australian Young Liberal Party, remember his name: Marc Dale. He's called for a boycott of the Body Shop franchise because the shops are selling Aboriginal armbands with proceeds going to an Aboriginal group.

The Body Shop says there is a demand among its customers to oppose the government's plan. Oh pish, says President Dale: we must punish a legitimate capitalist business for allowing its customers to express an opinion. Off with their heads! SHUT UP! Guards! Seize them! (Mr Dale is clearly on track to become shadow minister for business.)

The other guy being told to SHUT RIGHT UP is our governor-general, Sir William Deane. Now, this governor-general isn't a smug twit like Bill Hayden or a wild-eyed florid drunk running around race tracks frightening the chooks like Sir John Kerr. He's a mature, thoughtful gentleman with a bit of experience in the High Court department who reckons churches should be able to speak out on moral issues because that is their business, and that the reconciliation of Aboriginal and non-Aboriginal people in this country is very important indeed.

The Victorian Liberal premier, who gave his wife a government credit card, is eviscerating the independent auditor-general's office over the languidly timid squeaks of his invertebrate backbench and gives tax break after tax break to a casino part-owned by the federal treasurer of the Liberal Party, says Sir William is in danger of 'tarnishing his office' if he doesn't SHUT UP.

Heaps of people call this plan racist. And they're called 'extremists'. Give me a break. In other countries, when the indigenous people get shafted, they pop on a balaclava and start chucking bombs and shooting tourists. In this country they stay in the peaceful debate, appeal to reason and are supported by diverse community groups.

And don't get me started on Special Minister of Stating You Might As Well SHUT UP We're about to Pass Our Glorious Plan, Senator Nick It Minchin, or Tim 'Buckets' Fischer. I've got to get to the Body Shop before closing to buy all my Chrissie presents. Nerny nerny ner yourself, you big bullies.

# IT'S QUITE A BIG ARSE

Recently a columnist in another newspaper criticised the phrase 'a big ask' (meaning a difficult target), saying it was overused and mispronounced by sports commentators as 'a big arse'.

Sadly, until then, I always thought the phrase WAS 'a big arse', which was a crushing conversation stopper until I felt so much stronger about body image and so if anybody said (I thought) 'That's a big arse' I just smote them on the noggin with a handbag, or poisoned them. I also thought the crownheads of Europe were a German family who saw a lot of theatre. ('Performed for the Crownheads of Europe!')

Just as confusing was, 'Always the bridesmaid, never the bride', which I thought was an expression denoting luck, freedom and better frocks. Gradually it dawned on me— you're *kidding*—that people actually thought bridesmaids were MISSING OUT. Nobody ever clucked their tongue, shook their head and said mournfully, 'Always the best man, never the groom.' (I wonder if Zsa Zsa Gabor ever sighed, 'Always the bride, never the bridesmaid'?)

For the new Nobel peace laureates, Mr Jose Ramos-Horta and Bishop Carlos Belo, it was always a case of the rudely ignored activists, never the respected spokesmen for a decent cause—which is much more of a mouthful. Especially, it seems, for anyone who is now, or has ever been…an Australian foreign minister.

You can just imagine the scene in a few Canberra offices. Minion with Amnesty International report sticking to sole of shoe, smelling faintly of Fabulon, hurls itself into a random foreign affairs office. 'Sir, SIR, the Nobel Peace Prize has gone to some East Timorese!'

'Oh poop,' retorts the senior public servant, spilling his Krug, or possibly krugerrands. 'Double poop! That's only going to encourage the buggers! What would the berloody Norwegians know? Why don't they shut up and let us suck up to the Indonesians in peace! That's worthy of a peace prize, dammit!'

Former foreign minister Gareth 'Would you like fries with that, General?' Evans has been far more gracious, saying that the prize proves that the Indonesians didn't realise how widespread the global support has been for the East Timorese cause. (It can't be for lack of Gareth trying to tell them, surely.)

Gareth, of course, is in the running for the retrospective Nobel Prize for Moral Fibre in the Face of Glaringly Obvious Injustice Which Conflicts with the Odd Oil Deal, in which he is locked in a friendly tussle with the estate of a Mr Saro-Wiwa, late of Nigeria. This column is running a book on the result. If you wish to place a bet on Gareth, please kiss your money goodbye and place in a plain brown envelope.

Our current foreign minister, Mr Alexander Downer, has been nominated for the Nobel Rooly Brainy Prize, and will be coming out to lobby just as soon as he works out whether Bishop Belo and Mr Ramos-Horta are Portuguese, East Timorese, or Norwegian, and what our policy is regarding Norwegian refugees who have been shot at by Indonesian soldiers trained by Australians. In

151

the meantime Mr Downer has entered into the spirit of Scandinavian research. He told a journalist who penetrated his bunker with a howitzer and two tanks last Thursday that he's reading *Miss Smilla's Filling for Sner*, which he believes is about an unmarried Danish dentist.

Mr Downer is in good company with other nominees for the Nobel Rooly Brainy Prize, senators ex-minister Short and ex-parliamentary secretary Gibson who had to resign their positions in the government because they forgot to tell anyone they owned shares in companies which may be affected by their decisions. The official Liberal Party position on this is 'Oh, Christ.'

There is speculation that the prime minister should now insist that any ministers with shares place themselves in a 'blind truss'. This is not a bad idea. By blindfolding them and hoisting them by block and tackle in a truss above the crowds, any further confusing statements can be minimised. You have to be so careful with words.

# 7
# Mag Slags
# &
# Underbelly Telly

# THROW ANOTHER MAGAZINE ON THE BARBIE

An alert reader who is now having a good lie down has sent me a copy of *Barbie*, 'the magazine for girls', and what a treasure trove of absolute poop it is, too. Fun for all the family, especially if anyone in your family has expressed a fervent desire to look at prepubescent girls in full make-up.

Most girls go through phases of pink-frou-frou-please-let-me-wear-my-tutu-to-school (some of us never stop), and that's fine. The problem with *Barbie* is that it encourages this idea and no other. Crammed with hard-sell stories, it includes a beauty page (Australis lipstick $5.75) and a problem page (*Barbie* tells prepubescent insomniac to lay off coffee). There's a photo of a little girl wearing moisturiser around her eyes with glitter from the newsagent stuck on it ('Be very careful not to get it into your eyes').

Photography includes fashion pages full of little girls referred to as 'supermodels' with lipstick, sophisticated sexy hairdos and mascara. A ten-year-old looks over her shoulder in a pose that on a grown woman would be called seductive. On a little girl, it can only be described as deeply weird.

There's an article about wanting to be a lifesaver, with an interview with a nine-year-old nipper from North Curl Curl and 'celebrity lifesaver Pamela Anderson'. To be honest with you, Pamela isn't a lifesaver. Pamela is a woman with large pretend bosoms who works on a show called 'Baywatch'. (Coincidentally, there happens to be a new Baywatch Barbie available from the Mattel Corporation.)

There's some recipes for a Barbie tea party (Barbie tea sets available at 'your favourite toy store') featuring funny-face cupcakes with pink icing, pink smartie eyes and musk-stick mouths. *Barbie* magazine seems to see no contradiction in girls young enough to enjoy a tea party with dollies being instructed in come-hither poses.

The magazine hammers the idea that to be 'cool' and grown up is to look exclusively like the human equivalent of a funny-faced cupcake, not to mention a consumer. 'To keep your hair shiny and soft…try using Johnson's Kids No More Tangles Shampoo and detangler. It's gentle on your eyes [unlike glitter, one presumes] and smells YUMMO!' Ten-year-olds are not usually graduates of media courses. They don't understand that advertising poses as instructive editorial.

Little girls read these magazines on ideas for how to grow up. *Barbie* magazine does nothing to help them enjoy being a child, experimenting with any old dress-ups and different interests. Even in its nod to actually DOING SOME-THING—surf lifesaving—the role model is the closest thing to a human Barbie doll on the face of the planet. (Mattel might point to any Barbies dressed as doctors or artists—a commitment to provide diverse ideas or more outfits for sale?)

Scattered throughout the magazine are pictures of a twirling Ballerina Barbie (the only Barbie with flat feet rather than angled for high heels), a tea party hostess

Barbie centrefold, Barbie in a flouncy gown, Barbies in frocks and 'sports fashion', Baywatch Barbie, Hot Skatin' Barbie, the Barbie Sweethearts Pacific Pageant Barbie in a bikini and Cross-Dressin' Trucker Barbie with detachable pink facial hair. All right, I made up that last one.

The magazine ran a competition called 'Search for a Starlet' in which small girls were encouraged to go to a shopping centre dressed in a tutu or a pink dress. One six-year-old contestant interviewed for a cable TV show was asked 'Who do you think will win?' She replied, 'Anyone who's not fat.'

Thanks for nothing, Barbie, you dill-faced, dumb-shaped, hard-sell, plastic-extruded nong. Take Ken and your poxy magazine and CLEAR OFF!

PS: This column was used as part of an HSC English study guide for New South Wales school children. Question 7 was 'Why do you think Kaz Cooke invented the "Cross-dressin' trucker Barbie" with the detachable pink facial hair?' I mention this because I don't want anybody to feel that they may have got the answer wrong. I certainly have no idea.

# PICK UP SCHTICK

*Studio 4 Men* magazine has run a rather tongue-in-cheek story about a bloke who claims to be a 'speed seduction expert' and a 'pick-up king'. Ross Jeffries reckons you can get a woman into bed within twenty minutes of meeting her, probably snoring if you ask me.

He produces a newsletter called 'Get Laid!' with an exclamation mark and includes hints on how to 'nail' girls who just want to be friends.

Mr Jeffries uses hypnotism and the power of suggestion. For example, he uses phrases like 'feel happiness inside' which when said quickly sounds like there's 'a penis' in the sentence and other even ruder things that a work-experience girl like me shouldn't say.

Mr Jeffries believes these subliminal suggestions will, as *Studio 4 Men* magazine puts it so delicately, 'invoke in your victim an uncontrollable urge', i.e. to hurl herself at you and make like a crazed hamster. I think I speak for all women when I say that this would invoke in us an uncontrollable urge to fall to the ground in hysterical laughter.

# Don't Believe Everything You Write

There is a game called Chinese Whispers, so named because somebody begins by whispering something like 'Confucius say don't stick hand into light socket' into an ear, and after it has been repeated into many ears, the last recipient of the message is told: 'Confusion reigns when sticky hands make night rockets.'

And so rumours are spread, and so there are a few things I would like to clear up. Firstly, the New South Wales Minister for Consumer Affairs and Women, Mrs Fay Lo Po did not say on radio that it was only women who needed to hang their washing in the sun, and secondly, I did not tell Kerry-Anne Kennerley on national television that she was a dud root. Which one shall we clear up first? Oh, all right.

I was asked to attend a debate on the 'Midday' show about the worth of the best-selling book in the USA, called *The Rules*, which is a lot of absolute tripe about how to 'catch' a husband. Arriving at 'Midday', I found that my fellow debaters were a nice man called Brady something who proposed to his fiancee on national television and a lovely chanteuse called Maria Venuti. We all shared a dressing-room but given that we were already dressed, Maria's splendid form and her hat the size of Norfolk Island, it was easier for Brady and me to be in the hallway, where I refrained from asking Brady's last name, in case it was Bunch.

Anyway, we arrived on the set and hostess Kerri-Anne

showed the cover of the book and said that Rule Two is that you never ask a man out or ask him to dance.

'Kaz?' she prompted. Well, I was boned up. I had read the night before that the authors of *The Rules* conceded that a friend of theirs asked a man to dance and then did marry him, but he was pretty tentative about horizontal folk-dancing ever since (what with her shocking, emasculating behaviour on the dance floor, and all). So I said to Kerri-Anne, 'Not only that, but they reckon if you ask a man to dance he'll turn out to be a dud root.'

Within two days, people we'd never heard of from the Loire Valley and out the back of Rockhampton were ringing my parents to say I had said filthy things on the telly about Kerri-Anne's cotskills. Let me make myself completely clear: I'm sure Kerri-Anne's a right goer when the need overtakes her, but I'm only guessing.

Likewise, a few people jumped all over Fay Lo Po last week after she was on radio explaining why she wanted to change some of the strata-title rules which govern blocks of flats—in particular an end to the common rule against people drying their washing in the sun on balconies.

It was claimed that several times in the interview she referred to *women* wanting to put the washing in the sun and that, in the words of opposition counterpart Kerry Chikarovski, 'I would have thought [she] would be seeking to enhance the image of women, to move it away from being more than "just a housewife"...[this] reinforces the view only women should do housework.'

A reading of the interview's full transcript shows that Mrs Lo Po referred only to the deeply sensual right of 'people' to hang their washing out in the open air ('we all take pleasure in drying our clothes in the sun') until she introduced a safety element, the fact that 'if the owners of units don't make laundries safe where women might like to go and do their laundry and do it at ground level…and women want to dry their clothes in the sun then they are going to be able to do that.'

Fair enough. You never know who's going to be hanging around a basement laundry—a Chinese Whisperer, for example.

## LIKE ELLE, LIKE HELL

Elle Macpherson is on the cover of *Cleo* and the cover line says 'Elle's Body—Here's How.'

Well, I thought, this is going to be interesting! How can you go back in time, and get yourself born into the Macpherson gene pool, born to Elle's mum and dad nearly thirty years ago?

Unfortunately, it turns out to be an exercise program of push-ups, squats, reverse curls—which sound like a terrible perm experience—and thigh lifts.

Now, frankly, this is not useful. If *Cleo* had told us we could eat our way to looking like Elle Macpherson by eating twenty-five Tim Tams a day, that might be more interesting.

I'm waiting for the 'put-another-forty-five-centimetres-on-your-height diet'.

# FAT CAT CHAT

As usual, I'm looking for ideas on how to kill cats which come into my yard. So I figured with all the different magazines available there must be a cross between *Soldier of Fortune* and *Moggie Monthly*. Sadly, no. But I did find a copy of *National Cat*. And you would not BELIEVE the inside show-biz goss you can find in *National Cat*.

Under the heading 'Untacky Fat Cat's Back', the *National Cat* reports: 'Fat Cat faced a bleak life after being sacked from television but after five years in exile the famous children's character is back with a new act.

'Dumped for being too tacky for preschoolers, Fat Cat's return to the limelight proves he still has friends. Cat-minder Mandy Hunt said Fat Cat had been in Perth re-building his career.'

Now this is the kicker:

'He recently attended a teddy bears' picnic and had two bodyguards to protect him from hordes of young admirers.'

What is going on here? Bouncers with walkie-talkies batting the kids away from Fat Cat? The Fat Cat Armed Response Tactical Response Group? Or are Fat Cat's pants on fire?

Anyway, back to *National Cat*—there's a marvellous column by somebody called Bambi about a disease you can get from cat scratches or fleas which have been on cats, which makes you feel terrible for up to three months. I don't know why but Bambi doesn't suggest killing the cats.

But the rest of the magazine is surprisingly dull. It's full of pictures of cats who look like they've had their faces smacked in with a rolled-up newspaper and they never popped out again. These ones have names like Sublime Something Special, and its sister Sublime Special Charm, and Ish Blue Slink Swagman, a cat weighing approximately fifty-six kilos. There are also cats which look like they've been shaved and pegged out on the line for a couple of hours and these are called Devon Rex—now there's an ad here for a cattery specialising in these skinny terrified looking things and look who runs it: Pro and Rayleen Hart of Broken Hill. Yes, you've seen the ads: 'Mr Hart, Mr Hart, your cat has crapped on the rug again!!!'

## ARE YOU YOUR HAIR?

*Self* magazine, from where else but America, has an intriguing cover story this week. It's called 'Are You Your Hair?'

'Hair,' says the magazine, 'has a powerful effect on our moods and identity.'

And I think we can gauge the intelligence of the readers of *Self* magazine. When asked 'Are you your hair?', 72 per cent of them said yes. Probably 12 per cent of them thought they might be their knees, 15 per cent thought they were their toenails and 1 per cent screamed and said they were late for aerobics.

# CARTOONIST IMPOSTER SHOCK

Festive viewing in the traditional non-ratings period crap-telly season has been unusually rich, according to the telly publicists, who give thanks for the many new and diverting sitcoms from America.

One of them is called 'Caroline in the City', and is supposed to be about the wacky life of a female cartoonist. Being a female cartoonist myself, I thought I should give it a squizz and test its accuracy.

Caroline the cartoonist wears high-heeled white runners and white socks with a miniskirt. This is to indicate wackiness. In reviewing this outfit and its relevance to being a female cartoonist, I would have to say the costume department has made a rather obvious blunder.

Female cartoonists who work at home are very unlikely to have dressed themselves by the middle of the afternoon. Unless she has to go out and suck up to an art director or something, a female cartoonist, if she is wearing anything at all, might have popped on some stained track-suit pants, a pillowcase and her consort's Blundstones.

Caroline has a New York apartment with a drawing board in it, but in the episode I watched she doesn't actually draw anything. Nevertheless, she has a package ready for the courier—her cartoon for the newspaper and some designs for Christmas cards 'for the art department'. There are two crucial points on the matter of authenticity to be made here.

Firstly, if you do not do any drawings, it is very hard to put them in a package to send to the newspaper. If you put something else in the package, such as some folded up pages of *Greyhound Weekly*, the jig is usually up within a matter of hours, and you won't get paid. Also, if you give a courier an unaddressed package and say 'it's for the art department' your original cartoons are likely to be folded seventeen times, crushed almost into matchbox size, immersed in a mysterious ink and gravel solution and posted sea mail to somewhere in upper Zimbabwe.

In 'Caroline in the City', the perky young courier arrives on a pair of roller skates and makes funny comments, although sadly none of them are about the studied wackiness of Caroline's outfit. In my experience, a tired middle-aged bloke usually arrives in an un-airconditioned van, staggers up the front path and dispenses hilarious witticisms such as 'Gidday. Gotta parcel, love?'

The episode I saw was actually about Caroline's friend, a tortured male artist who briefly pretends to be gay so he can be paid lots for his paintings in a gay art gallery. The subplot is that Caroline has two-timed her hairdresser. Caroline's best girlfriend is a standard kind-hearted slut, although she never seems to actually have sex. Caroline's boyfriend is a man who is rude to her friends and doesn't notice her new hairstyle.

After ten years as a female cartoonist, it is my considered opinion that circumstances are more likely to be arranged thus: Caroline would never seem to actually have sex or notice her own hairstyle, her boyfriend would be two-timing her, she'd have a gay best friend and a tortured hairdresser who is a rude slut.

Still, a new year is a time for optimism. Perhaps someday Caroline will get into her pyjamas and draw some cartoons.

# MEANINGFUL NUDDY WORK

We're still going on about it. Everybody is creeping into the newsagent and putting their vegemited fingers all over the *Black and White* magazine's nudey musicians issue. Don't spend the $25—take it from me, the only person in it over size 10 is Dave Graney and IN 248 PAGES there's not a single tummy banana in it.

Here are the highlights. Some people have revealed too much about themselves:

Tim Finn, for example, is far too sophisticated to get his gear off—he's opened his shirt and says in his interview that he greatly respects the music of the Pacific. To illustrate his immense respect for Pacific culture he has been photographed with a gaggle of island women with no tops on, lying around as if they've just done four hours in the cot with Tim. You're not fooling anyone, sunshine.

Likewise a dance music artiste called Dara who flings herself about a hotel corridor with her legs in opposite directions, claims in her interview that she's a 'feminist' and then reports that her new single is called 'Use Me'. Hello? Room service for Miss Dara. Sign here, it's a reality cheque.

I have been through the whole edition with a microscope and can report that most of the people with a successful career haven't bared everything—except poor old Christine Anu and Angie Hart from Frente. Your agent might tell you it's tasteful, ladies, but you're now officially in a stick magazine.

Singer Nikki Costa explains, 'I'm cool with being naked, as long as it means something.' Accordingly, she's been photographed with ASS written on her arse in case anyone thought it was her ELBOW.

# BUT WHERE'S THE LITTLE BALD BLOKE?

First thing I learned about Christians is that they have insomnia.

'This Is Your Day with Benny Hinn' is on at 5.30 a.m. on Channel Ten.

I was really waiting up for 'The Benny Hinn Ministries', mostly because I thought it was going to be a church run by Benny Hill. Benny thanked viewers for chipping in $5 million for phase one of his own TV station, and interviewed father-and-son pastors called Ron One and Ron Two (presumably Ron Three was at home doing some bib work) and they prayed on a waist-high stack of financial documents.

Benny believes in fasting and asks us here in Australia to send money, or possibly Tim Tams. You can buy a $70 package of power prayer so that your prayers go straight to the throne room of heaven.

Benny performs exorcisms on stage, but it's a bit of a production line. He rattles through a few people with Parkinson's and osteoporosis—and he touches them on the forehead and they fall over and lie there. It starts to look like a slumber party on the stage, so he gets a guy called Doug to come in and clear up.

Then he gets to the headliner healing: one woman with the well-known virus of having demons (is there a Medicare provider number for demons?). She's lying on the stage with four people holding her down.

Benny: 'Hold her boys, the devil's coming out of her. Come out of her, come out, come out of her...I love it when the devil's come out.'

Lordy.

# SECOND PRIZE IS A DATE WITH
# DR FRANKENSTEIN

*Woman's Day* is offering a competition for which the prize is a new body.

Has it finally happened? Has *Woman's Day* given in to their macabre obsession with corpse-snatching à la Dr Frankenstein?

No. They claim that if you win, you get to choose either three months with a personal trainer or one session of liposuction, a surgical procedure that is too revolting to go into here.

The competition-offer is illustrated with a model dressed as a responsible member of the medical profession—i.e. a complete dork in a white coat with what appears to be a light gaffer-taped to his head. I'm not making this up, apparently *Woman's Day* thinks that modern surgeons are kitted out like coalminers. The pretendy doctor is holding out a stethoscope, presumably to check whether the lucky liposuction patient is, like, still breathing.

But the bit I like best is that the doctor-model is featuring an insane grin, and brandishing a handful of scalpels and a pocket full of scissors. This is most reassuring.

This surgery prize idea is clearly a brilliant move, and it can't be long before *Woman's Day* is offering more exciting medical procedures as prizes. Worried about your legs? Why not draw attention from those problem areas and have your ears grafted onto your knees! How about an unnecessary kidney transplant, or another quick and simple way to lose weight, a gratuitous leg amputation.

As a matter of fact, bugger it, I've got nothing to do next Monday, I think I'll have a hysterectomy. Good on you *Woman's Day*.

# VET DREAMS

The host of Channel Ten's new animal show, 'Totally Wild', Katrina Warren, has done a fashion shoot with animals for a magazine. She's photographed in a strapless evening gown accessorised with a border collie and a stethoscope. She wears a leopard skin print and diamond earrings to bandage a cat and, my favorite, a fake monkey fur stretch velour plunge cleavage top and miniskirt—just the thing to wear when you're having a squizz down a dog's ear canal. She'd be a hot date, wouldn't she? 'Ready to hit the clubs, Katrina?

'Yeah, I'll just finish inseminating this aardvark and pop an injured vole in my clutchpurse. I'll be right with you!'

# DRIVING MISS OOPSY-DAISY

Those of you who shared the astonishment at Ford, which produced a car called the 'Probe' that only a gynaecologist could want, will be thrilled to hear that there is also a car called Starlet, and what wanna-be foxy lady won't be driving that around?

It's been quite a car-ish week, with an invitation to the launch of the new Volvo (I didn't go, but I think the new Volvo is called 'The Volvo') and a report in *US Car and Driver* magazine by John Phillips about the names of new cars, including the Mitsubishi Mini Active Urban Sandal.

Sadly, the car will only be called that in Japan. We'll probably have to make do with the Mitsubishi Thong. Other names recorded by Mr Phillips at a Tokyo trade show include the Mitsubishi Debonair Exceed (in Australia this will be known as the Stuart Wagstaff Two-Door), the Mazda Proceed Marvie (we'll call it the Mazda Not Bad), and the Subaru Astonish!! (perhaps this will be re-named to reflect our more low-key culture and become the Barely Raised Eyebrow Twincab).

Enough of cars and on to something more important—the 17,000 stories about the Royal family. Princess Margaret wrote to Fergie and told her to bugger off—in fact her exact words, according to the *Daily Telegraph*, were, 'How dare you discredit us like that and how dare you send me those flowers.' Perhaps she wanted a packet of fags and a bottle of tequila instead.

The Duchess of York is all over the joint, with Reuters

news service referring to her rather melodramatically as 'The Flame-haired Duchess'. If this style catches on, we'll be having 'Edward, the prematurely flouncy-haired fleshpot prince', and 'The Queen Mother, a sparsely thatched greying temptress'. Anyway, the Titian-haired romp-mistress has been betrayed in a new book by her former clairvoyant (Imagine! A dishonest clairvoyant!) who taped their conversations.

The raven-haired clairvoyant claims the vivacious red-headed siren wanted Kevin Costner and John Kennedy junior and didn't get either of them (a situation not unknown to millions of women in the western world, incidentally) and that, according to *Woman's Day* (*impeccable* source), Fergie stripped off and demonstrated a sex aid to Princess Diana, the brooding blonde bombshell.

What Madame Whatsherface the psychic didn't seem to reveal was what kind of 'sex aid'. With the English upper class, it could have been an orange, a stout riding crop, a servant instructed to shout 'I'm Charlotte Rampling! Spank me!', or a Land Rover tow bar. Who knows with them?

Everywhere there are lurid royal rogering romps. *New Weekly* magazine (*excellent* source) reports that poor old Princess Stephanie of Monaco is a tad depressed after seeing pictures of her new husband with a young lady who was awarded the title of Belgian Miss Tits in 1995. ('I'd like to thank me parents and, of course, Phillippe, who does the block and tackle work.')

Then the tabloids got onto a mousey-brown thatched Captain James Hewitt look-alike who was playing film horsey with an actrine pretending to be the pouting fair-haired Her Ex-Royal Minxness. The *Sun* newspaper in London admitted it had been duped by 'cunning fraudsters' which certainly sounded better than 'We fell for an obvious scam'.

According to *Woman's Day* (a source), Camilla has moved into the Balding Would-be Tampon's country estate and 'has taken control of the servants'. As you would. The *Daily Telegraph* says this ambition to give Camilla, the grey-blonde-haired-fiendishly-flicked-backy-kind-of-hairdo person, a more public role has forced out Charles's private secretary, Commander Richard Aylard, a man who probably parts his hair on the left, who had urged more discretion.

Also in the women's magazines are some pages of celebrity photographs called 'What People Are Wearing'. Let me kill the suspense here and now by revealing that people are wearing clothes.

I hope you've been paying attention, because there'll be a test on all this later. (It's called the republic referendum.)

# You Can Never Be Too Rich
## or Too Stupid

An important survey has fallen into our pertly manicured hands: 'The Beauty Behaviours of Top Australian Women's Magazine Editors', by Dr Debbie Then. Now, in case you think we might be inventing Dr Debbie Then, she is a 'social psychologist' and, her resumé says, a 'speaker, writer, TV presenter health, beauty, sex, relationships'. But perhaps not a punctuator.

Dr Debbie's resumé says she 'regularly offered commentary on the "E!" entertainment television show during the O. J. Simpson trial'. Possibly she regularly offered her thoughts on the jurors' hairdos? Dr Debbie is, however, revealed as a smart cookie—sorry, no American-isms—a canny iced vo-vo, with her idea for the study.

In June, she polled the 'top 25' (huh?) Australian women's magazine editors about their beauty and fashion habits. These women pump out exhortations to the lumpen cellulitariat to buy more clothes, get a new lipstick, do step aerobics all week long and have surgery on our earlobes. Wouldn't it be great if they really lie around in flanny shirts, tracky dacks and blue eyeshadow, swigging warm sherry from a plastic cordial flask and screaming for a feature on the firmness of Goldie Hawn's botty?

Only eight of the editors answered Dr Debbie's survey. All women, the editors' average age was thirty-six, their average pay was $63,000, and they spend $10,000 a year each on clothes.

Get up off the floor, we haven't finished yet. 'Unfortunately,' concludes Dr Deb, they don't get clothing allowances, so 'Australian trendsetters must use their own money to fund their stylish habits.' (Amnesty International will be informed.)

All respondents wear lipstick every day, feel attractive and—odd, given that the magazines bang on about it constantly—only 13 per cent wear sunscreen (13 per cent of eight editors is, what, oh never mind, surely Dr Deb knows what she's doing, she's got a PhD), and only half have dieted. Seventy-one per cent worry about their weight, probably because they've been looking at the pictures of Year 5 models in their magazines. Get this: '37 per cent regularly wash hair off their upper lip and chin area.' Was it stuck on with Clag? Their chin hair WASHES OFF?! Now, that's a news story.

Asked by Dr Debbie to explain why women's looks matter, responses ranged from the political, 'we're trapped in a patriarchal society', to structural engineering, 'that's they way we're built'. The editors define big fashion crimes as wearing high heels with pants and wearing too few clothes (as in: oh root, I've gone out in only my gumboots and wiglet *again*).

Variously, the editors are most confident when 'my hair is behaving' (Down, Flossybits, down!), when they're having regular sex, when they have a good haircut, or relax with friends and feel well-informed. By which we can deduce that the most confident women's magazine editor in any room is the bouffed one reading the newspaper and having sex while her hair is being subdued by a pal.

Some editors didn't practise what they preach. 'I wear black clothes and brown lipstick,' wrote one, confessionally. 'I don't exercise,' says another, '[and] other editors I know wear no make-up and many of us smoke.' 'Well, I bombed Sarajevo,' said another. (Okay, that last bit I made up.)

Asked for weight-loss tips, one brainy editor responded, 'Stop eating.' Dr Debbie filed the following under her report heading: 'Did She *Really* Say That?' Asked if a woman can be too thin, one replied: 'Only when the bones are protruding and you're not getting your period.' And, oh, maybe if there's some difficulty getting a pulse, or something.

Dr Debbie concludes that, 'For all their seeming glitz and glamour, magazine editors…are approachable, and they are concerned about helping women with the business of looking good. And that is a subject we can never learn too much about.'

Can a woman ever be too learned about beauty and fashion? Only when the brains are protruding and you're not getting your clothing allowance.

# A LOAD OF ARTY BOLLOCKS

I wasn't going to touch the controversy about the 'fashion' pages in *Juice* magazine with a 10-foot model. Then I saw an article by the *Juice* editorial director defending the pictures against critics—and then I saw the photos of 'Fashion to Die For'.

Mr Toby Creswell wrote that images of male and female models pretending to be bashed, strangled, overdosed and otherwise murdered was a 'concept...developed by the photographer, editor and art director as a means of presenting a fashion shoot that avoided the cliches and standard representations of clothes and models'. Come off it.

This 'concept' has itself been a cliche for years from *Harpers Bazaar* to *The Face*, from ads to Tarantino movies. (It was the next big thing after photos so blurry you couldn't see the clothes.) The genre includes models made up to look dead; pretending to be dead; as assault victims; or chained or bound. What's next? Maybe taking pictures *after* decomposition has started—although make-up advertisers would probably whinge, and it would slow things down considerably if the models' lips fell off every time they pouted.

Mr Creswell has a few good points. The photos are unlikely to cause copycat youth suicides. (A teenager is unlikely to bash himself to death in a gutter while wearing an $825 suit for a start.) Mr Creswell says using dead people to sell things is common, and *Juice* is unfairly singled out. He mentions Nick Cave's recent 'murder' album (the 'everything Nick Cave does is cool' defence?) a bank ad and the 'ER' telly show—although 'ER' doesn't usually pop a patient into a half-slip, rumple it up, photograph her to suggest she's been raped, killed, and dumped in a paddock and call it arty fashion.

Mr Creswell says he recognises the dangers of glamorising anorexia and, accordingly, *Juice* does not 'encourage images of emaciated, disempowered women'. In the *Juice* photos, there are images of three thin women who are all dead—which is fairly disempowering. You can't tell if the fourth dead woman, 'Black female age 23' is thin or not because you only see her from the waist up, drowned in the bath with an articulated shower cord around her neck and an exposed breast. Come to think of it, she does looks a wee bit disempowered.

Mr Creswell also complains that some people called the piece 'heroin chic' and says rather huffily that 'none of the models in our shoots are in any way associated with heroin'. He's right. The young woman depicted dead of 'respiratory failure due to poisonous substances', in perfect glamorous make-up and a revealingly arranged spangly gown is shown with spilled pills and capsules, some red suede shoes ($350) and an empty bottle of Czar Vodka (presumably not big advertisers in *Juice* magazine). Has the model just found out how much the shoes cost? Or was the fashion crew thinking about the most common tool of suicide in young women—and how it's best to die wearing something halfway decent. (Personally I felt some well-placed vomit, faeces and rictus might have made this look a bit less of a glamorous way to go, but what do you expect of a fashion shoot? Reality? Well, don't.)

Mr Creswell says his 'little pictorial' has done its job by stirring up a debate about violence and women and anorexia. Pull the other one, if you've got one. Why not just admit nobody thought about it that deeply? If the fashion industry was an emperor it would be in the nuddy. One recent newspaper fashion story said, 'Barrie's approach to fashion is down to earth: "Clothes are clothes. You wear them, throw them on the floor and have them dry-cleaned."' (After Barrie's serving minions have collected them with gold-plated tongs, presumably.) But let's be fair. Mr Creswell may exercise his right to print stupid fashion pages and defend them. Even if it's a load of old bollocks.

# 8
# Playtime

# CAKEWALKING TROUNCEMEISTERS

Last week my baseball team lost a game forty-six runs to zero. There are many metaphors, aphorisms, similes, palindromes, aerodromes and when-in-Romes in that for a writer, but quite frankly all I want to say is that the whole thing really sucked.

What usually happens in baseball is that you play short innings, in which one team bats and the other fields until it gets three batters out. In our case, we played one innings where the other team hit balls over fences and into other postcode zones for nearly one hour, then we batted for seven minutes, then the other team batted for practically the length of the seventeenth century and then we batted for a nanosecond before it was 'time and game'.

We had eight players, they had nine. They had matching socks and a lap-dancer on drugs by the look of it. We had two rookies, a Pomeranian-cross terrier and a struggling pitcher. (Our pitcher, Georgina, struck out one batter in the whole game and we all nearly wet our knickerbockers.) They said things to their players like, 'Come on Charmaine, finish her off' and we said stuff like, 'Try and hit the ball', and 'Kill me. Kill me now.'

Thousands of men, women and children in this country play weekend sport and many of them know the agony of defeat. Few know the added frisson of total humiliation. (FORTY-SIX-NIL!) Mindful of Tom Hanks's coach character in the girly baseball movie *A League of Their Own*, who shouted 'There is no crying in baseball!', we didn't cry out there on the diamond, which, by the way, was looking less of a girl's best friend with every passing runner visiting first base for a cup of tea on her way to home plate.

We remained stoic while our opponents (a Division Two standard team) tonked, smacked, whacked and mashed the baseball over the space of just over two hours. Meanwhile, we Division Four standard volunteer lambs attempted to get them out. Here's how.

At one point I stood under a fly ball, hit high into the air. 'Mine!' I shouted, a baseball convention used to warn off any of my colleagues with the ability to actually catch the ball. I stood positioned under the ball, my glove outstretched. 'I got it, I got it.' The ball, which was fitted with some kind of remote-control device invented by the CIA, fell a good kilometre and a half behind me.

One of our outfielders, Mimsie, took the opportunity to have a little sit-down at centre field, which is where I found her after running into the outfield to chase the ball. Did I say, 'Are you well rested, Mimsie?' Did I say, 'It might be better if you tried standing up, Mimsie, it would give you such an advantage next time the ball is hit somewhere near you'? No, I did not. I simply pointed out, 'Mimsie, you are sitting on your f— arse, for God's sake.'

I apologise. It was the strain. At that point I believe the score was thirty-four to nothing, although when the score is 34–0 and there is no end to the game in sight, the score might as well be 140,000 zillion² to nil, because that is what it feels like. A creeping, inexorable despair washes over the entire team, and players begin to have individual hallucinations about freezing to death in the Antarctic.

Or, of course, you could be part of the sort of team that refuses to be daunted, pledges a single-minded passion to win, pulls itself up by the bootstraps, buys in some great players, bribes the umpires and generally turns into a raving bunch of SAS-trained winning machines.

I am not part of that sort of team. I am part of the sort of team that had a beer after the game and swore a lot. But you never know. Mimsie's trying to get Tom Hanks's phone number.

A while ago the well-paid lunkhead and majorly dud date Mike Tyson got into a boxing ring in the required fury, bit part of Evander Holyfield's ear off and spat it on the canvas. In the boxing world this is considered very bad form.

It is the correct etiquette, instead, to batter a bloke about the head until his brain turns to trifle. Surrounded by older men who have been your gurus since you were a confused teenager, which wasn't that long ago, men living out their dreams through you, you may punch somebody repeatedly in the eye with the force of a car accident until blood comes down in sheets. Top night!

We worry about boys who are uncommunicative suicide risks, and men full of anger who bash their mates, girlfriends or family. Then we pop the boxing on the telly and the big pub screens. Here's the measure of a man, lads. Try and beat the shit outta somebody. How come you're not that muscly? How come you're afraid of things when these guys talk so tough? What's the point in talking when belting someone makes you a rich hero or a gold medallist?

A blow to the head tears blood vessels between the skull and the brain and causes bleeding. Too many times and you're brain-damaged. Too much at once and you're dead. A career in boxing can cause dementia or Parkinson's disease (Muhummad Ali's problem). Boxing should be called Intentional Injury.

Supporters of boxing say there is a risk of injury in any sport. This is perfectly true. However, the principal aim of soccer is not to cause massive internal bleeding in the opposing team. Generally speaking it is considered super-fluous to the contest for a 400-metre butterfly swimmer to break her opponent's nose and punch her head until she has brain damage and a disfigured face.

Like many boxers before him, young Queensland amateur Lance Hobson died last year of a brain haemor-rhage the ringside doctor said was caused by a punch during an official fight. Lance was trying to support his family. His parents said they didn't blame boxing. Nobody asked boxing whether it blamed his parents.

There are other ways of giving kids discipline, self-respect and anger management, getting them fit, keeping them off the streets. Other ways that poor kids can imagine a decent life: free education and full employment, anybody?

Doctors want kids discouraged from boxing by dropping it from the Commonwealth Games and the Olympics. (An outright ban on all boxing would just cause secret fights, some say.) It's one thing to tolerate privately funded brutal spectacles run by the likes of Don King, that venal Ameri-can with hair like a paintbrush in a wind-tunnel, but why are our tax dollars promoting boxing as a sport? Perhaps it's because of the superior intellectual skill of boxing's Olympic official, the particularly hilarious Mr Tunstall.

Boxing commentators said convicted rapist Mike Tyson was 'chicken'—he bit Holyfield because he couldn't punch him into unconsciousness. If only Tyson had brains enough to be 'chicken' years ago and walk away from the whole thing. 'Tyson Is a Disgrace' said the headlines. No, you wackers. Boxing is a disgrace.

# THE DIFFERENCE BETWEEN RUGBY AND AUSTRALIAN RULES

## HOW TO TELL AFL FROM RUGBY

Whoever said that rugby was eight guys trying to push seven guys up one guy's bum had it only half right. The guy with the bum (called the hooker, I ask you) is shortly thereafter instructed to chuck the ball to the 'second rower', who places the ball on the ground, stands on it, and has a think about rowing while several men try to kill him.

Everyone on the field has a cup of tea and makes polite inquiries about the mothers of their opponents, then the rower passes the ball and the sugar to a half back who gives it to his cousin, usually a ring-in called Jonah Meninga with a body not unlike a refrigerator on legs, who runs to the end of the playing field with opposing players chasing him to try and get up his bottom. If this plan fails the opposing players will engage with all of the other players on the field in trying to stand on Mr Meninga's head at once. Relatively little of this happens in AFL. (Also, AFL players do not find it necessary to gaffer-tape their ears to their heads in case of fire or theft.)

In AFL, there are eighteen players per side on the ground at any one time, an interchange bench, goal umpires in lab coats, boundary umpires in shorts, field umpires in melees, a couple of doctors asking questions of concussed players: 'Who's the Minister for Telecommunications?' 'Humphrey B. Bear.' 'Close enough: play on, son'; three messengers from the coach per side, a couple of stretcher-bearers, a few photographers, reporters, love-struck fan clubs with huge run-through banners, physiotherapists, aromatherapists, police, the bloke with the oranges, a streaker, some timekeepers, a couple of travel agents and somebody trying to find his dog.

There are forty-seven sirens at various times during an AFL game. Many of them are called Lorraine. They brush their hair in the stands and try to lure the players onto the rocks—in this case, out of bounds on the full.

## POSITIONS

Rovers are the zippy gypsies of the game, able to play anywhere on the field. Ruck rovers are like rovers except that they are taller and have nicer haircuts. Wing men are men who like wings. 'Hello,' they say, 'I used to be a leg man, but now I'm a wing man.' (Wing men have terrible trouble picking up girls.) Okay, the only other position you really need to know about is half forward. This means a player might have to be encouraged, unlike a full forward, who may have to be warded off with a hatpin.

Full backs are the der-brains of the game, and have the bad luck of constantly being given the job to mind star full forwards. 'Sit on the bastard,' says the coach. 'Stick to him like glue.' (Sitting on a full forward's head is as close as the game gets to rugby, and rarely proves an impediment to the work of the full forward.)

You may hear some loose talk about flanks and pockets, with regard to position on the field. The players call themselves a 'back pocket' because they do not want to be mistaken for a handbag. This, quite frankly, is an act of sheer paranoia, because if you cannot tell the difference between an AFL player and a handbag, you are a wee bit peeper-challenged, and what's more nobody is ever going to ask you to the Brownlow Medal dinner.

BARRACKING
Compulsory. At various times during a match, you may shout 'Baaaaawwwwlll!' which is an instruction to the full back that he is now allowed to cry 'Holding the Man!' a gentle reminder to players that although organised sport is one excuse for allowable physical cavorting between men, things can only be taken so far, and 'Go, Swans!' which will do for all occasions including the ballet.

# AUSSIE RULES PANTS ALERT

I speak of the glorious day at the MCG yesterday. I speak of the magic of Michael Long, the rhinoceros-like grace of Ryan O'Connor, the endless bad-hair day of Peter Everitt, the way Glen Coghlan stood so close to James Hird that most of the time you could only see his bootlaces.

But the main game was not the main game. The main game was the Ozkick with the little tackers at half time. The game with a crying rule which approximates the blood rule—i.e. if somebody makes you cry you've got to leave the ground and get a cuddle.

There were all sorts of kids out there, girls who went in like Micky Martyn, girls who were chatting to the seagulls instead of watching the ball. Little boys who kicked goals and little boys who cried when they got knocked over by a galumphing six-year-old three times their size. But they all had one thing in common—their dacks were falling down around their ankles. As many of the ankle-biters discovered, you can't play a blinding quarter of footy when you have to hang onto your duds with both hands for the entire time! You might be able to get away with it in soccer, but not AFL!

You can't concentrate when you've got your hands full of your strides. The AFL and sponsor McDonald's must act! Either provide shorts the right size, sew the duds to the jumpers or gaffer-tape the dacks onto the tinies! Years ago crowds used to yell out 'Holding the Ball!' Now they just say 'BALL!' Let's not get to the point with Ozkick where the combined mighty roar of the MCG is: 'SHORTS!!!!!'

PS: A few weeks after this I went to a game at Waverley. The half time kids were playing in shorts the size of hamster pants. Will they never get it right?

# Francine Panto to the Rescue

It has been necessary to attend Francine Panto's Beauty Therapiste Salon of Joosh, Foof and Buff several times a week to gain some respite from the worst of the Olympic Games commentary. (If I have one more facial peel you'll be able to see the back of my head and next week I'm getting the soles of my feet waxed.) But sometimes a gel (as an equestrian commentator might say) has to escape.

Some of the Olympics commentators make as much sense as Alexander Downer. As a concept. (Incidentally, there's a rumour about that Mr Downer thinks he's the foreign minister. Go figure.) An ABC radio announcer described a shooter's demeanour on his way to a gold medal as 'almost contemptible', which seemed rather mean-spirited until one realised he may have meant contemptuous, or possibly languid, or vulpine, camp or bossy, who could tell?

The telly commentators at the softball insisted that runners were 'tagged out at first', or 'run out at first', which is roughly equivalent to a commentator of world-class cricket saying a batter had been 'fouled on the stumps'. (A softballer is 'thrown out' at first base, an expression rarely used by commentators in case anyone gets any ideas about their own employment.)

Further to the women's softball, two commentators, both of the bloke persuasion, consistently called foul balls 'fly balls', whether they went high in the air or not. But the true zenith of professionalism was reached when a young blonde woman from Newcastle came to the plate, preparatory to mashing the ball through the infield for a glorious, intelligently placed safe hit. 'Won't she be marketable if they win the gold medal,' drooled one, who sounded a lot like Drew Morphett, warming to his theme and banging on about it for some time. For brevity's sake, he could have just said, 'Phwooooarr, eh?' We would still have got the message.

Another play was said to be a 'third baseman's dream', unless of course you're a person of the girly persuasion on third base. They remind me of the legendary American baseball catcher Yogi Berra, who was asked by a school teacher after a failed exam: 'Don't you know anything?'

Mr Berra replied, 'I don't even suspect anything.'

Instead of going to the beauty therapiste, some people avoid commentary by doing their washing for the first time in four years, and discover that there's a function on their washing machine called Bleach Inlet, the perfect name for a new Australian soap about a couple of blonde extras from 'Baywatch' and two blond Olympic beach volleyballers who get washed up on a deserted inlet (natch) and eat a couple of boxing commentators they find wandering around in the hinterland shouting things like, 'Get the ref an optometrist! The Australian boy has probably sustained irreversible brain damage by now, but kerist, is he PLUCKY!'

And speaking of a touch of class, I think the highlight of the Australian coverage of the Olympic Games (apart from the fact that you don't see footage of anything much without a Nozzie in it) has to be the equestrian commentator.

Her name, from memory, is the Hon. Lucinda Fforkingtonshire-Smyth Pot-Arsed Snorking Perkins Riley the Third, and she was a total trimmer with a Prince Charles accent. 'Have you got any idea what's going on?' Stan Grant would ask.

'Yes, frightfully,' Lucinda would begin. 'Thet's Melissa Gullytrap on Tickety Boo Velour Loungesuite, a rahly mahvellous gel, with a terrific mount, never rahly been orn a horse before, but demned game, and as she takes her iting rind the course, oh my giddy ornt! OOPS-A-DAISY, she's demolished the fence. Now, that's morked as an error, sadly. But she's a heart as big as a hice, well, my hice anyway. I expect you live in rather a small hice, Stan. She's broken forty-eight bones but she *will* stay the course, and I think that says it awl abite equestrian events.'

Stan to camera, 'On ya, Snorkers.'

# DORKSPORT

All summer long we are forced to be spectators at dork-sports in the news. Dorksports are not, generally speaking, normal sports—not even the absurd lengths some champions and Olympians go to for their sport necessarily makes them dorksportspeople.

Our leading synchronised swimmer trains for eight hours a day, for example, which brings it perilously close to the realms of dorksport, but not quite there. Synchronised swimming would be a dorksport if there were saltwater crocodiles in the water, it was croc-mating season, and the swimmers thought they were doing something worthwhile.

The essential dorksport elements are lone pursuits or small groups, the probability of really serious danger and a stupid, reckless disregard for facts, other people and the ineluctable forces of nature. A bonus aspect of dorksport is causing danger or major inconvenience to other people.

Skiing downhill playing touch footy in the dark? Dork-sporty. Solo round-the-world yachting? Definite dorksport. Getting whole navies out to look for you, and people to risk their own lives trying to save you, is approaching dork-sport nirvana. Many dorksport participants call themselves adventurers but are really losers with money.

The bloke who just put his hot-air balloon down in a Russian paddock will now try to circumnavigate a planet in a speed boat. Somewhat surprisingly, his chosen planet is Earth. The guy is simply an all-rounder dorksportsman and one imagines he is a big fan of road luge.

Then there are the dorksportspeople who simply drive everyone crazy with the utter pointlessness of their endeavour and desperation to feel like they're a bit special and interesting. Trying to get up to the top of Mt Everest in a blizzard. Swimming from Cuba nearly to North America covered in some kind of gel which looks like custard, being stung by jellyfish, smashing against the side of your shark cage, exhausted, hallucinating, sobbing and begging to get out of the water while your parents keep yelling at you not to stop. That right there is known as dorksport by proxy.

Somehow, Antarctica brings out the dorksportsperson in people. I don't know whether they just think, 'Penguins can hang out down there, the show-offy little bastards. I'll show them!' or that triumph of logic in the answer given when asked why they attempted to ride a BMX across the Sahara ('because it's there') or because they think they look sexy in a parka. But, for some reason, Antarctica does it to them.

These are the sorts of people who say they respect nature and then proceed to ponce along to the South Pole for no particular reason, getting major frostbite which no doubt is then treated with the help of our taxes. 'Oh yes, bits of my thighs are falling off and I've lost an ear or two, but I walked to the South Pole and so I'm a bit fascinating.' No, mate. You're a dork.

There were few survivors of the summer's attempt by a group of dorkskydivers to land on the ice in the Antarctic with the temperature at approximately minus a zillion and no visible horizon.

When it's dorksport versus Mother Nature, put your money on the Mother.

# BRIGHT LIGHTS, BIGGISH CITY

Now that I'm a Melbourne girl again I can only gaze upon the majesty of natural beauty that is New Zealand and say to you for Christ's sake, why not get somebody to build you something nice, such as a completely enormous casino complex with parking for 5400 cars.

Just as the new casino in Melbourne squats over King Street like Kerry Walker having a wee in the bush in *The Piano* movie, the Auckland harbour could be straddled by a hotel tower in beige-style concrete cladding, and still leave room for some pink travertine toilet blocks and a few thirty-seven-storey carparks on Bastion Point.

I can see the planning meeting now. 'Somebody tell the Maori mob, they'll be all right, we'll give 'em a few free tickets to the floorshow. Get onto it, would you Trevor… where's Trevor gone?'

The thing is, once you've got the casino up and running, it becomes the landmark—forget about your other points of interest. Melbourne is now so totally domi-nated by the casino conglomerate (sorry: Crown Entertainment complex) that other attractions are dwarfed. Next to the neon-explosion of the casino, the elegant purple-lit spindly Arts Centre spire is going to look like a discarded syringe. Captain Cook's cottage might as well be the outdoor dunny.

Whatever you do, make sure you go bigger and better. We've got half a million square metres of floor space; 2500 gambling machines; 350 gambling tables. Nerny ner ner, to paraphrase premier Kennett. Fourteen cinemas all showing blockbusters! Thirty-three shops including the sort of boutiques with $4000 handbags! Planet Hollywood! Allstars Sports Bar! A car park for 5400 cars! Restaurants! Nightclubs! A twenty-six-metre video screen!

And remember that taste is important. We've got the hot-pink Velvet Bar for instance. Gold-plated loo plumbing. The Asian-themed Diamond Room, the Monte Carlo Room, the Las Vegas room still to come. The miserable bastards who just did their life savings room. Sorry. Made that one up.

It's just that the estimated cost is $2.3 billion and if one is a pernickety old slag, one might wonder how much money people are going to have to lose in the joint to pay for it?

Still, as the premier said, don't be afraid of change. And a couple of old mates playing whist round the card table won't do any more.

We're talking glitz, glitter, showers of chandeliers and precision waterfalls. We're talking seven-minute-cycle repeating light shows which use enough gas each time to run the average house for a year. We're allegedly talking an eighty-metre Italian marble wall that the boss didn't fancy so a crystal wall's been whacked up in front of it. We're talking huge jets of flaming gas ejaculating repeatedly into the night.

We've got deeply attractive billboards, full of ads for Red Hot and Rhonda, a Las Vegas style floorshow at the casino with a tall woman called Rhonda Burchmore, a stage full of dancers, and a fair bit of sequin and bum-feather type arrangements, by the look of it. There are billboards featuring Rhonda, a significant part of whom be legs.

One billboard around the corner from my place has been artistically enhanced by somebody who has placed the head of a giant, green three-eyed monster where Rhonda's used to be. If this was in the show I would consider popping along. Oh all right, I wasn't invited. Not on the A-list. Not, if you wish to be technical, even on the Z-list. Dissenters have been disappearing all over town.

Excuse me for a moment, I hear a rather insistent type of battering ram at the front door…

# THESE KNEE-SOCKS WERE MADE FOR WALKING

I'm going to have a wee stomp on the Melbourne casino because nobody else is. I'm just going to deliver a wee boot up the bum to the sort of people who go to those exclusive shops at the casino hotel complex and buy $4000 Prada handbags and $10,000 Chanel knee-socks with emerald sprauncing panels.

I mean there IS such a thing as going too upmarket. The prices at the casino boutiques are enough to make anybody fall laughing to the floor of the Donna Karan shop, going the projectile vom right down the front of a darling little mint-green velour safari suit with detachable diamond epaulettes and a date with Adnan Khashoggi, the Sultan of Thing.

For example, Daryl Somers is pictured in *TV Week* in the HUGE new casino entertainment bit describing it as 'tastefully opulent'. I myself'd say there's been an explosion in a chandelier factory. Daryl is holding a martini apparently paid for by leaving four silver and three gold Logies on the bar. Unless he paid for his drink with an Oscar and that's his change sitting there for the next round.

I realise that the new casino cost 567 gerzillion trillion dollars and it has 117 cinemas and gold dunnies for Kerry Packer and Christ knows who's going to pay for Red Hot and Rhonda and Jeff Kennett to be shot into the air in flames on the hour, but enough's enough!

Give Daryl a drink and let him keep the damn Logies.

# GADGETS FOR GIDGETS

Does one really need a banana lounge with lino-layer option and goatee-trim attachment? Is one's life incomplete without plug-in sprauncing tongs with a free frittata recipe book? Of course not. But will we buy them? Will we what—it's summer sales time.

The shops are as well-packed as Mr Darcy's white strides in the TV version of *Pride and Prejudice*. On the first, most deranged day of sales, one would be well advised to take bottled water, a snake-light, a couple of ockie straps and a picture of yourself in case of existential crisis.

For getting through crowds it's best to be equipped with a replica orange plastic Gatling gun, spiked shoes (with the spikes protruding from the sides, like the ones on the chariots in *Ben-Hur*) and a cut-price Splayds set picked up early on in the melee. Some people camp out for days beforehand, spending their Christmas bent over a primus singing 'Kumbayah' in front of the shop doors, and they are PUMPED.

By the third day the shop assistants have seen every indecency committed by rogue members of the general public, and they are punch-drunk and query-shy. I was looking for a food processor which would dice, slice, and otherwise suffice. 'You don't want one of those love,' said one in the kitchen appliance section of a big department store, 'it's got all these stupid, fiddly bits that nobody uses. It'd drive you mad. Fair dinkum, it's bloody hopeless. Hopeless. I'm telling you, it'd be a disaster in your kitchen.' Okaaay.

'Now we've got your lovely deep fat fryers here, $1.50 off the reccy retail. You just chuck anything into it and it comes out covered in fried fat. It's a brilliant concept. Hot lard-covered anything in minutes. When you've finished you can just throw it over the parapet to repel any would-be castle invaders, or pour it down the sink and completely root the aquatic environment, it's entirely up to you.'

This is the main problem with the sales: the items that have been reduced in price are either gone by 10 a.m. on the first day or they're stuff that nobody else wanted to buy for reasons which probably have some merit, for example it's complete crap.

In the manchester department, after using a mega-phone to sing 'Volare' while standing nude on the head of a legless mannequin for three hours, I finally attracted the attention of a sales assistant who looked like he'd been in an emergency ward for a couple of days. 'Are any of the pure cotton sheets on sale?' I inquired lightly.

Suddenly I was swept from my perch by a short, stout woman wielding a bazooka, an umbrella, and forty-five parcels. She leapt onto the sales assistant with a terrifying cry of 'Kowabunga!' and wrestled him deftly to the ground, straddling his chest. 'Not again,' he murmured faintly.

'Excuse me, I was first,' I said. Her eyes turned into red Christmas lights and her head revolved. She spat at me, 'Ye painted spawn of Beelzebub! Ye must fall back under the righteous glance of mine gorgonlike orbs, or pay with your spiritual fluids!'

'On second thoughts, after you, sunshine.'

After she had been directed to flounced valances and valanced flounces, the assistant turned to my original inquiry. 'Don't be a ninny,' he said. 'No cotton sheets on sale. On sale are plastic sheets, hessian pillowcases, doona covers knitted from buffalo grass by ill-paid Asian persons and I think we still have some blankets carved from nuclear waste in the bargain bin.'

A subsequent trawl around the music section revealed that anything by Phil Collins, Kenny somebody and the Singing Nun was reduced by about 586,000 per cent. There was a *Best of Racy* CD at 79 cents and the double album set of *Bryan Adams Belts Out Your Favourite Unspeakable Banalities* was surprisingly reasonable. Just the thing to pop in your new deep fat fryer.

# KIPS

There's nowt much more sus than politicians and high-powered businessmen who claim they can get by on about three hours sleep a night. No wonder the joint's in such a mess. And it's not like most of them have a good excuse, like 'I'm breastfeeding' or 'I was at a rave party' or 'The guy next door plays the French horn a lot'.

Take Bob Dole. These last few days of the American election campaign, he's lurched around the country like an unwelcome cadaver at a slumber party, making much of being able to function on no sleep and even less in the way of policy. Journalists asked him ponderous stuff about what it was like to look like a loser, instead of asking the obvious, 'Why don't you go and have a kip, you dozy bugger?'

Shakespeare once said something about sleep knitting up the ravelled sleeve of care, or unpicking the sleepy seam of woe, or crocheting the vests of the insane gentlemen of Verona, or something. Anyway, what Shakespeare is saying (a phrase which ricochets endlessly through any English class, to which the weary student replies, 'Well why didn't he say so then?') is have a good lie down.

He was trying to tell us that if Lady Macbeth had only tried the odd afternoon nap she wouldn't have ponced around the battlements in her nightie at all hours, trying to rub the imaginary soy sauce off her hands with an imaginary Wettex, and if Mr Macbeth had gone to bed early he wouldn't have been buggerising around a paddock in the middle of the night with a bunch of nutty witches who invented newt soup. Well that's what I wrote in my HSC exam, anyway.

Shakespeare would not have been impressed with that small, merry band of taxi drivers who offer one a No-Doz and a Jolt cola as they hurtle along with two wheels on the footpath boasting that they've been awake since about 1978 and it's never done them any harm at all. (This last phrase is usually delivered mid side-swipe at 500 kilometres an hour on a roundabout going the wrong way round and singing along to John Laws. While he's not singing.)

There is, I am told, some sort of design fault in small children which compels them to wake up at 6 a.m. and bounce on your bed. Perhaps this fact could be more widely publicised as an adjunct to contraception information campaigns. Babies, one is aghast to learn, will wake up SEVERAL TIMES A NIGHT, sometimes crying their heads off. This is the height of rudeness, and has led to the perceptive comment that sleeping like a baby is hardly to be recommended, and possibly was the source of the concept, 'Sleeping with the Enemy'.

There is just not enough sleeping, napping, kipping or shut-eye going on. A friend has recently discovered that he has a sleeping disorder which resulted in him waking up thirteen times an hour. He discovered this because he spent a night in the sleeping section of the hospital where they wired him up to this snore-ometer thingie and registered his brain waves which were completely berko. He now has to wear a little mask for a few weeks which will help him breathe properly, and then he'll be cured. The hospital could have made the mask look more like the Phantom's than a bondage jockstrap for the noggin, but anything's better than waking up thirteen times an hour, unless it's listening to John Howard.

Nursery story characters were always nodding off— Goldilocks, for example, and Rumpelstiltskin. Sleepy was clearly the only one of the seven dwarfs with a grasp of reality, what with every morning going 'Hi Ho Hi Ho it's off to work at the unidentified mine with only a pick axe and a funny hat'. No wonder they wanted somebody to do the housework. And if I was Sleeping Beauty I would have taken a cricket bat to that interfering Prince who woke me up.

# 9
# Time Orf

# TOURISM BOON TO APPLE ISLE

When one's paramour, the mightily talented wiglet-maker to the stars, Mr Des Tiny, spirited one away on a Fokker Friendship, initially causing a fracas at the travel agent due to a mispronunciation by a passing Hungarian interested in aviation, one had time to read up on one's destination.

Due to the languid progress of the Fokker, one had time to study approximately 278 travel guides on one's destination (Nemrut Dag, a mountain in Turkey: one's beloved has an ambition to visit every place in the world with *dag* in its title) and also to read up on every destination in this part of the solar system, including the Mir space station (one and a half stars).

One was captivated (not least by Mr Tiny's crocus-coloured crushed velveteen parachute pantery) by the concept of what foreign persons might read about one's OWN national parts—so one embarked upon the perusal of a locally produced tome about Tasmania, that happy isle to the south of, well, everything else.

The publisher of said tome was rather brusque with Mr Tiny at a cocktail soiree a few weeks ago to launch the *Australian* magazine.

Mr Tiny had politely inquired whether the publisher would be interested in husbanding Mr Tiny's delicious eight volume verse-novel about living in the wild with a tribe of interior decorators in a small but perfectly formed suburb of Hobart. The publisher, of *Supercilious Guide to Your Map of Tassie*, glared at my be-sequinned babe and intoned nastily, 'I hardly think your little trip would be interesting enough to scribble on the back of a Liberian airmail stamp for domestic usage, you little worm.'

Well. Later that evening, cleaning the Salmon Surprise out of one's foundation garments, removing a waiter from part of Mr Tiny and patting his black eye with a hearty lamb chop (they always have steak in the movies, but hell, book contracts don't grow on trees) one decided to tour Tasmania anyway with one's main squeeze in a Humber Vogue and a matching set of diaphanous brunch-coats. (One shall attempt to run a two-bar radiator out of the cigarette lighter on the dash.)

At this Arcticky time of year it still costs a farm and a leg to get to Queensland from where we are, but the Tasmanian Tourist Bureau offers 'Desperation Packages' and 'Beautiful One Day, Hailing Like Buggery the Next' tours for $7.50 each and a free Porsche Spider if you get on the boat to Devonport. If you promise to spend a Saturday night they will pay off your mortgage.

Anyway, what one is trying to say is that the *Supercilious Guide* has Tasmania down as a bunch of redneck sexist backwoods bonkers who discriminate against the nancier portions of our close-knit community. Well, that's out of date. They've repealed the law against gays and not before time, as Mr Tiny has pointed out. How on earth they thought they were otherwise going to attract the big musicals so essential to a state's economy, one can't imagine. One shall report one's findings forthwith.

# CHEESY HISTORY

'You have eaten all of the brie on the island. Get out!' the fey sergeant shouted, as the Tasmanian Cheese Police threw me on a plane. Meanwhile, my paramour, Mr Des Tiny, was dragged away by a bevy of big-boned Taswegian minxes wearing cramp-on bootery, Tassie tiger tights, and smirks.

Before that, the holly was jolly. We saw a deeply enticing sign near Swansea which promised 'FOLK ART, MANURE'. It was near the Kabuki restaurant, where the host brandishes a picture of a cross-looking Amanda Vanstone if you try to pay for something little with a $50 note. It is very frighty. We did scream and scream.

The Dick Betts Gallery in Hobart had a fab exhibition of somebody's response to colonialism and the way Poms painted Oz wildlife, using chook-wire and paintings and feathers—it was strange and clever and beautiful. The artist turned out to be a sixty-three-year-old lady called Irene Briant and I want to be her when I grow up. Another guy had been taking brilliant, kaleidoscope-like photos of the inside of the world's great high domes.

As luck would have it somebody has cottoned onto the fact that there's some stuff in Tassie you can't get else-where. That's why the tourists go. This includes real wilderness that hasn't been woodchipped or flooded or otherwise completely rooted, and real old towns—not the ones with Ye Olde Authenticke Jointe Scones $8.50 signs.

As Des and I stood upon a boat deck being lashed by nought per cent pollution, 456 trillion knot winds (which refers to how many knots it will put in your hair) horizontal sleet and bits of Macquarie Harbour being blown up our fleecy-lined witches britches, we reminded ourselves, during a spot of al fresco Morris dancing, what a jaunty time the convicts here must have had, what with being starved, flogged, chained, worked into the ground, bashed up and given rags made out of thin calico to wear once a year.

'Hurrah!' they must have shouted every so often. Thankfully, this jolly view of history is continued in a booklet for kiddies about the child convicts. No black armband history here! (Not unlike the *Spirit of Tasmania* ship's diorama which says that 'sadly' the languages of the Tasmanian Aborigines are 'lost'. Damned careless blackfellas. Not only did they all commit auto-genocide by throwing themselves on guns and insisting on being locked up in a disease-ridden concentration camp, they've misplaced their languages.)

The *Peter Piper Picked a Pocket* activities book sports a rosy-cheeked grinning convict tyke playing marbles and learning to read. Not for him a sadistic flogging or solitary confinement on bread and water. (See Robert Hughes' *The Fatal Shore* for the real deal.)

Can't we just look back and admit that really awful stuff happened? That people treated other people with cruel, vicious contempt, official and otherwise? Because if not, we can't say we're kind of improved.

Now we've got ideas and a mix of great art and cultures and people who are teaching their kids that racism sucks, and some attempts to reconcile the past. THAT'S how you can tell there's been progress. Also, there are more cheeses now.

# NO CAPITAL IDEAS

No wonder the people in power in Canberra think things are tickety-boo any way you look at them. No wonder they think families are a combo of the Waltons, the sit-com Cosbies and a vat of cash. Hurrah, fresh air, everything's so quiet and neat and clean—either concreted or manicured or set upon by gangs of ambitious architects with edifice complexes. Nobody is in the streets laughing, talking or fighting.

Have you ever been to Canberra? It's a theme park called Boring World. Where everybody drives shiny new cars around new roads with landscaped roundabouts and those perfectly flat velvety lawns.

Sure, there's some cool stuff in Canberra, like the country's official art collection and museum and library—but here's the catch. You have to go to Canberra to see them. Amid the world of New Food, and the food of the New World, Canberra is congealing custard on stale jam roly-poly.

Where we live, there are gangs of rellies pressing clothes and putting them in drycleaner plastic, language schools, boutiques, derros, and ferals with purple hair. Blokes in overalls. Blokes in frocks, sometimes. Point is, there's lots of different people. Beggars, wankers, mums, dads, rich, poor, and the in-betweenies.

Canberra, as far as a visitor can discern, is populated by a total of 152 people, all of whom wear new clothes, look as comfortable as a brown cord beanbag, and send each other outdoors in parties (not the fun kind) of not more than four people at a time. Canberra looks like a 'smart bomb' went off—one of those brainy devices which kills all the people and leaves imposing national monuments untouched.

On a sunny Sunday the lake is almost deserted—ten public servants with hairdos roller-blading, one old bloke in a regulation Canberra-issue cardie and a golden retriever. Want to take over Australia? Land a small rowboat, a rude person and a megaphone on Lake Burley Griffin. It'd all be over in minutes.

Unless the big ejaculating fountain went off at the wrong time, or the invasion was startled by the pissy pealing of the carillon clock looming out of the lake like a particularly hideous multi-storey car park for Fiat Bambinis, marking time by neurotically going off every five nanoseconds.

Canberra looks like a posh or comfy middle-class suburb in any big city. And if most of the members of parliament come from the same kind of suburbs, THIS is what they think Australia looks like. On the face of it, an entire huge boring suburb of fully employed, housebound Mormons with no taste in architecture.

Bugger the argument about Canberra being a waste of space and that the capital of Australia should be Sydney or Melbourne. Politicians should be forced to meet in an Aboriginal community (without fresh water) forced off its own land to make way for cows or British nuclear tests. Or a town or suburb anywhere where the big employer, the hospital or the hopes of the young people have been 'downsized'.

The problem is the politicians can't run, but they can hide.

PS: To be fair, Canberra has many tourist attractions. One of them is a scale model miniature English village. There is a kiosk.

# CANBERRA REPLY: OH MY GOD

It has been some time since anybody around here has been able to mention the word 'Canberra' without certain columnists gnawing their way through the floorboards and refusing to come out.

The editrix thought it would be a good idea to reply to the letters of complaint about the column on Canberra recently. By way of raking over the excruciating subject, let us recap the series of events.

1. Your correspondent goes to Canberra for the weekend and finds it looks very dull and boring. She writes suggesting that *on the face of it* (her emphasis) it all looks very comfy and shiny and fully employed and no wonder some politicians who hang out there think everything is 'relaxed and comfortable'.

Your correspondent remarks that Canberra's lake area being so deserted it looks like a so-called 'smart' bomb (named by the Pentagon) went off, killing all the people and leaving the buildings standing. She files her contribution four weeks before the magazine is due on the streets, not knowing how much she will come to regret the metaphor or why.

2. The *Australian* produces its pre-printed magazine, and stores it ready for distribution.

3. A Canberra hospital demolition implosion goes horribly wrong, scattering debris over the lake area, killing a girl and injuring other people.

4. The magazine is inserted and distributed, several days

later, in the Saturday edition of the *Australian*.

5. Many people, believing that the correspondent is entirely bonkers and trying to make jokes about the tragedy, write very upset and furious letters to the editor and the correspondent. A brief explanation and apology appears in the letters column of the *Australian* during the following week.

6. Several other people write to say that Canberra is a vibrant and fascinating city full of unemployed people and the correspondent ought favourably to consider a physical relationship with the nether regions of a deceased bear.

It remains only for the correspondent to further state that she feels sure that Canberra has many kinds of people living there under various economic circumstances. But when you visit Canberra you do not see this. There is no evidence of this in the tourist precincts. I'm sorry but Canberra does LOOK boring.

Letter writers explained that Canberra has the highest level of sports participation and volunteer workers, and that many people have lost their jobs, with more losses to come.

The correspondent wishes it to be known that she was trying to have a go at politicians who take things at face value, not the people of Canberra, and that furthermore she passionately despises early deadlines and their consequences and reminds readers nationwide to ensure they attend the free Canberra Floriade Festival each year in September and October, the biggest floral extravaganza outside of Sweden, which is COMPLETELY DIVINE and even prettier than Canberra in autumn. For God's sake tell them I sent you.

# HOT CROSS RELATIVES

My grandfather used to sit his girls down at Easter time and try to impart something of the majesty and power of faith, even if it was a belief based on something he hadn't seen. 'Jesus couldn't have come down to earth from heaven,' he would explain. 'It's light years away—even if he left 2000 years ago the bloke wouldn't be here yet.'

With that kind of loose talk in the family, and a paternal ancestry with the religious motto, 'Aintcher never took a risk?' the home where I spent much of my formative years was a swirling tumult of atheist thought underpinned by the tenet best explained as 'Yeah, whatever you reckon. What's for tea?' (Chops.)

Easter was particularly confusing, with its mix of pagan bunny-worship and egg hunts and buns with crosses on them, some sort of festival of gluttony, and something to do with Jesus being born, or dying, or doing something with a lot of fish sandwiches.

When I looked at an icon of Jesus wearing the crown of thorns and bleeding, on the wall of a friend's house and said, 'Mummy what have they done to that poor man?' she told me the story. It was presented as a sort of Amnesty International homily about what happened to communist-leaning political dissenters wearing a beard and a caftan. With the proviso that I treated it with the same intellectual rigour applied to the matter of the Princess and the Pea. (For some time I was concerned that if Demis Roussos voted for the Labor Party the Romans would crucify him.)

Some time afterwards it was decided that my brother and I would attend Sunday school with the express purpose of broadening our minds and getting us out of the way on Sunday mornings. We stuck cotton wool on pictures of the Holy Land to represent clouds and attended church with twenty cents for the plate. I came away with the impression that it rained a lot in Israel and the church didn't have enough pocket money.

I could relate to the confusion of the Japanese department store which mounted a Christmas window display of Santa Claus on the Cross. There was particular difficulty with the concept of God being Jesus as well as dead (father, son AND the Holy Ghost) as well as being Jesus's dad and Mary being his Mum. I felt that this left Joseph in a rather precarious position and it was fortuitous that there were three wise men on hand for counselling. And where did the reindeer fit in?

This was further complicated by the revelation that God was everywhere, had made the entire world, and Jesus Christ was what grown-ups said when they hit their thumb with a hammer. The result of all this was that I was disabused of the notion of a real God before I heard the tragic news about the Easter Bunny and Santa Claus being, well, something that we just pretended for the smaller tykes.

Some people performed mysterious rituals at Easter time instead of going camping. This involved eating biscuits that were the body of Christ and drinking wine that was actually his blood and led to the inescapable conclusion that Jesus was basically holy leftovers.

The most religious person we knew was a nun who gave us piano lessons. I used to think that the piano seat was part of the habit, hidden under the folds. She was, it transpired, actually married to God, or possibly Jesus. I couldn't believe she didn't have any wedding photographs. Talk about a missed opportunity.

But even with this intensive atheist training, I can't forget that Jesus is still light years away, possibly hurtling past the Hale-Bopp comet. He could be here any minute. With his views, for his sake, I hope he doesn't land without notifying Amnesty International.

# ALL HAIL THE QUEEN

You can just imagine one's tremulous ecstasy when Floozita di Spanken rang and asked one if one would accompany her to the Queen's Birthday drinks at Government House.

Even though, as a committed Queenophile, one knew that it wasn't Her Majesty's REAL birthday at all, one fully concurred with the implication that a celebration of such a felicitous event was better late than never.

One set about wondering what does Prince Philip give the Queen for her birthday? The poor bloke must think every year: 'She's got racehorses, a gigantic Royal yacht, enough jewels to sink it, some very nice hats, Canada…' (Rumour is, last year he tried to buy back Fiji as a surprise but Colonel Rabuka wouldn't be in it.)

Anyway, the invitation said lounge suit or day dress. The wardrobe yielded no day frock for temperatures below the swelterish so it was basic black trews and jacket with a cameo brooch featuring a portrait of the Queen herself with little diamantés attached to represent a tiara and necklace.

It transpired that some people had interpreted 'day dress' to mean full-length extinct fauna coat, hats akimbo and some rather extraordinary military dress uniforms with about fifteen metres of gold cabling draped come-hither style over the manly chesty bits. Sir-woooon!

It was the hottest date one's been on since a Northern Territory Supreme Court judge took one to drinks on a

Japanese navy ship. (The judge warned that some people might look askance at this, one being considerably more nubile in those days, and he being your distinguished, rather chronologically more experienced person. 'Don't worry, Judge,' one said, 'I'll just tell them you're my toyboy.' There was a short delay while we all explained what a toyboy was. You can't say the judiciary isn't getting an education in wider cultural mores.)

Anyway, as we all milled around hors doovering and drinking champers out of Marie Antoinette's bosom glasses in a splendidly appointed ballroom and some naval hunks tootled on their woodwinds in the balcony bit, one could imagine that it wouldn't be a bad gig, this Governor business. The velvet banquettes are just the thing for a bint to languish in, batting her eyelashes at whoever takes her fancy, as Floozita herself discovered, having forgotten to change out of her pyjamas before she arrived.

The toast to the Queen, one felt, was disappointingly brief, i.e. 'Ladies and gentlemen, a toast to Her Majesty the Queen.'

'The Queen!' people shouted gaily. One tried to say 'Hurrah!' but people stared. One would have preferred something a little more comprehensive, detailing some of Her Majesty's more incandescent qualities.

Anyway, one has decided to run for Governor at the earliest opportunity. One shall invite you to ALL the garden parties. Also kick-to-kick on the Lawns and any Official Languishing.

# CHRISTMAS PHOBIA

At least one capital city has started a Christmas phobia group, which is just outrageous. Phobias are supposed to be irrational fears—but fear of Christmas is perfectly sensible. And besides, if fear of the number thirteen is triskakeidekobizzothingiephobia or whatever it is, fear of Chrissie would have to be SanctusNicolaiphobia or something.

Christmas is the most stressful time of the year and I wish everybody many happy returns. As if. Only the kiddies are happy at Christmas. For them it is just a cornucopia of battery-operated-'tis-better-to-receive-than-to-give type arrangement which lasts for hours until they stick a few D-cell batteries up their ear canal or get into a fist fight with the cousins over tippety runs and are off to Christmas Casualty.

'And who was Jesus, darling?'

'The man whose name Mummy says when I did put Muffy in the microwaver with the puddin'.'

It's not that I'm a Scrooge about Christmas—I wish it WAS all sweetness and light beer. But sadly, for most people, it's a time of wondering why their family doesn't live up to the images in the department store Christmas ads, where each toothy soul gets a humungous present and there's a hell of a lot of twinkling—not all of it from the Chrissie lights.

And the human rights violations!

Gigantically insensitive rellies saying things like 'you're

putting on a bit of blubber there, girly' to adolescent girls who are growing normally and will continue to do so unless terrifed into fat phobia, martyred women shooing the men out of the kitchen and transforming themselves into Christmas drudges: preparation, serving, cleaning up, kitchen sherry, coma.

Women being given battery-operated kitchen appliances! Small children getting violent shoot-em-up battery-operated thingies with huge merchandising agreements tied to telly shows! That simply appalling paper millinery! Malfunctioning crackers! The jokes of uncles! The effort it takes to hide a lifestyle from conservative relations, even during lunch! Cold custard! Kids finding out about Santa!

Christmas cricket is always a good idea, whether full backyard rules, tippety runs or beach cricket. Get in for some action before everyone sits down for the next seventy-two hours to watch other people doing it. When I was little I thought the Boxing Day Test was an exam the day after Christmas to see how much we'd all taken in.

And if you don't have any around the place yourself, you can borrow a couple of kids for the day: there's more excitement than a red-lemonade festival, and the fascinating sense of being instructed on international disputes in microcosm.

'That's mine!'

'Is not!'

'Is so.' (Whack, whack, whack, sounds of sobbing.)

I'm bigger than you!'

'My Dad runs the U. N.'

'Well my mum says your Dad is a no-hoper who couldn't find his own bum if he had a street directory.' (Repeat until bedtime.)

Well, each to their own. If you're religious have a Mary Christmas, if you're bearded, have a hairy Christmas, and if you're gay have a fairy Christmas. And happy new year to all!

# THE A TO Z OF CHRISTMAS

ANXIETY

This is the natural state of Christmas. Ranging from 'Whose present have I forgotten?' to 'Exactly what will be the consequences of Uncle Bazza giving the kids plastic flamethrowers and three kilos of red-food-dyed lollies?'

BON BONS

These are pulled before the traditional luncheon, providing the assembled company with essential bad jokes, plastic whistles and gaily coloured paper hats, a talking point for people who have nothing else to say to each other because they're related.

CREDIT CARDS

Best to cut them into teensy pieces right now and save the bank the trouble of doing it for you in the new year.

DRUNKS

And drinking. Plenty of both. From this time on beware of people lurching down the street in front of you, launching themselves off the curb in front of your car at green lights and accosting you at every party. Leave if you hear the triumphant cry, 'You bewdy, I've found another bottle! It's banana advocaat—let's rip into it!' This also applies to creme de menthe, blackberry nip and methylated spirits, and anyone who wants to run their Y-fronts up a public flagpole.

EDIFYING SPECTACLES
See above.

FAMILY, DYSFUNCTIONAL
Don't fall for the TV sitcom style of perfect family ideal at Christmas. Statistically, you're far more likely to have several people missing from the equation, a great-aunt who tries to seduce your boyfriend under the lemon tree, a cousin who arrives on a mixture of angel dust and battery acid, an uncle who chooses pudding-time to announce that he's had a radical change of sexuality and a father who tells the entire mob what a bunch of no-hopers they are.

GIFTS
Some families choose to buy presents at a set price for a lucky dip, others go into debt, some go for the most unromantic ones possible. 'Well darl, I noticed the couch grass was getting out of hand under the Hills hoist so I got you a lovely whipper-snipper.' Sometimes you will be given a present that convinces you that your family has NO IDEA who you are, for example you get a pale-blue fluffy toilet-seat cover. The correct response is, 'How splendid! I hope you like the Anthrax album, Aunty Glad.'

HAM
This traditional fare is served once on Christmas Day either hot or cold, and then provides enough salmonella sandwiches well into February.

I
Interminable internecine interfering intermeddling; intolerable, intoxicated, introspective, introverted inturges-

cence; involuntary invective; irritating, irascible idolatry; illuminating ignominy, impoverishment; Invalid Port invoking impotence; innumerable inflicted infamous innuendos; inundating, interrogative, incivil inquiries; indiscreet indulgences; indefensible incidents and inordinate indignance.

## JESUS

This is the whole point of Christmas. Three wise men were tooling around the desert on their camels when they saw a star in the East and decided they should follow it, as you do. When they arrived, they found that a young couple called Mary and Joseph had been refused service at a hotel and had a baby in the stables. The wise men arrived with regulation nativity scene kindergarten towels on their head and gave some presents to Jesus which included gold, frankincense and myrrh (batteries not included). Jesus turned out to be God's, and he grew up to be a very nice bloke indeed with a line in catering miracles. He was murdered but didn't really die and went back to heaven (Easter). Many books and speeches occurred over the next 2000 years trying to explain the whole schemozzle.

## KILOJOULES AND KISSING

Be warned that some people will hang a piece of mistletoe as an excuse to try to give you a big tonguer underneath it. The best way to avoid this impertinence is to pretend you're about to be sick as a result of kilojoule overload.

## LAST-MINUTE SHOPPING

God's way of reminding you what hell might be like. This travesty is designed to put stress levels off the dial and re-introduce you to the idea of peace on earth and love for fellow humans, along the lines of, 'Excuse me, I was here first, get out of the way you cow, there's no need for headbutting sir', and 'Excuse me, I've been running into my own reflection for seven hours, please point me to the nearest exit of this department store or I shall be forced to assault you with this industrial-strength length of tinsel.'

## MARTYRDOM

Women with pointedly long-suffering expressions of simmering resentment will have slaved for fifty-six days making mince pies, shortbread and handmade streamers, then put on a clean pinny and cook a hot lunch for 420 relatives and a salad incorporating the regulation ingredients (iceberg lettuce, canned beetroot, canned pineapple, boiled eggs cut in half and no-brand mayonnaise). They will then wash 7689 dishes, a process which takes approximately as long as the ice age. For their pains, the women may be told, 'Good on you, Val' unless everyone else has gone to sleep or is out the back playing tippety runs.

## NON COMPOS MENTIS

Literally, not master of one's own mind. Can happen at any stage of the Christmas experience, most often during last-minute shopping, after cooking the lunch or after being harassed about one's lifestyle by a relative you're not supposed to be rude to.

## OBSTETRICS AND OCHLOCRACY

If you are pregnant, try not to have the baby on Christmas Day. Your child will thank you for avoiding a lifetime of combined birthday-Christmas presents. Ochlocracy, or mob rule, is the state immediately following the opening of the presents by young children.

## PUDDING
Part of our proud English heritage when servants were rewarded for a lifetime of slavery by finding a sixpence in the Christmas pudding. An early form of enterprise bargaining.

## QUEUEING
Even more so than usual at the post office, unavoidable at department-store cash registers and around the block at bottle shops.

## RUDOLPH
By this stage you will be completely jack of Rudolph and his less nasally challenged colleagues Donner, Prancer, Blitzen, Sneezy and Grumpy. You will not wish to hear anything more about the feast of Stephen, want to be right away from a manger and have a fervent hope that the people singing 'Silent Night' would take their own advice. If you are trapped in an elavator before Christmas you may have contracted muzakitis and need Professor Carol Suppression's Academy of Rhythm and Blues Therapy.

## SPRAY ON GLITTER, SILVER AND GOLD PAINT
By this stage the less occupied in the family group will have gone completely Tonia Todman and sprayed everything in sight, including little bells, plastic sprigs of holly, front-door wreaths, baubles, pine cones and slow-moving infants. Why pine cones? Nobody knows, but it is believed to be the same craft school which put about the rumour that cotton-wool balls looked like snow.

## UNCTUOUS PROGRESS LETTERS

Some families send out little stay-in-touch letters with their Christmas cards, enumerating the incandescent achievements of their family members throughout the year. A typical sample: 'Jeremy had a marvellous year at Grammar, making the first eleven, getting honours in his exams and if it wasn't for the tiresome distraction of those arson and possession charges in September we feel sure he would have retained his position as Fagin in the class production of Evita.'

## VALIUM, PROZAC, LITHIUM, TEQUILA, MARIJUANA, SEREPAX

Stock up now to avoid the rush.

## WAIFS AND STRAYS

Many families include a waifs-and-strays element to the Christmas function, which can see you making conversation with an exchange student from Zimbabwe who doesn't speak English, the homeless guy from the bus stop who doesn't speak Sober, or somebody who nobody wants to speak to any more, like Pauline Hanson.

## XYLOPHONE

And all other toys which make discordant, whirring, siren, plinky-goddamn-plonky, shrieking, whistling, banging, ringing noises. If you have children involvement on the day, these noises will be burned into the central cortex of your brain by 9 a.m. Rearguard actions can be mounted towards the middle of the afternoon when all batteries, hammers, sticks, bows and arrows, air rifles, ground-to-air missiles and Follow Me Home and Flatten My Bosoms Barbies are confiscated.

## YAHOOS, YABBERING UPBEAT RADIO ANNOUNCERS AND YO-YOS

These may all be avoided by a) avoiding Bondi, b) not turning on the radio and c) accepting that they don't seem to sell replacement yo-yo strings any more.

## ZUMBOORUK

The *Shorter Oxford Dictionary* defines zumbooruk as a small swivel gun, especially one mounted on the back of a camel. Clearly, by today's standards, the three wise men were foolishly under-resourced in the bazooka department.

# 10
# Lucky Dip

# Reasons to Be Cheerful.*

1. Thongs: as footwear, icon, or insect dispatcher.
2. A relatively low number of reported alien sex-linked abductions in your area.
3. The idea that if you hit it over the fence, you're out.
4. The fact that a national hero can be called Nugget.
5. Aloe vera, or eucalyptus-impregnated tissues. Can Prozac-hankies be far behind?
6. Souvenirs made from kangaroo scrotums must be inspected by quality control.
7. People can write rude letters to the editor under false names.
8. The miracle of tulip bulbs.
9. The way John Howard and Kim Beazley both send everybody nigh-nighs practically as soon as they start speaking.
10. You can drink absurdly hued cocktails in funky bars and snort when you laugh.
11. Most women are not compelled to wear the sartorial equivalent of a horse blanket for allegedly religious reasons.
12. The way men kiss, fondle, pat and then homo-erotically wrestle each other to the turf on weekends in a manner they would never consider off a sports-field while anybody was looking.

* From an idea in the *New York Times* magazine 6 July 1995 called 'What's Right with America', which included 'quilted toilet paper', 'hiking boots as urban style development' and 'Rocktober'.

13. The vast majority of our primary food products are not available in a spray can yet.

14. Rural women still make the best pavs in the known universe.

15. The Spice Girls' publicist lives in another hemisphere.

16. Australian Rules.

17. Kissing like you mean it.

18. Some places are going back to their musical Aboriginal names instead of being called colonial era things like 'Completely Lost Gully' and 'Mount Utter Hopelessness West'.

19. People who are afraid of boring lives call their children things like Melliinda and Jar-Edde.

20. There might be a plan afoot to photograph every man who goes to a lap-dancing strip club for lunch and publish their pictures in the *Women's Weekly*.

21. You're not an emergency staff member of the Mir space station.

22. Eventually everybody will be skint and they won't be able to go to the casino any more.

23. Jarmies with little racing cars on them.

24. If you wanted to, you could get a beehive hairdo and hide stuff up there.

25. Advances in marketing: there is a chemist product called Anusol.

26. At Christmas time, you can sing 'dashing through the snow' prostrate on sand in 38-degree heat.

27. You're not expected to fully understand the Bosnian situation.

28. When stilettos come into fashion, only the very

young wear them, and then they're out again, and nobody ever gets sucked in two seasons in a row except fashion writers.

29. Not every Nazi gets a visa.
30. Coffee is legal.

# A Wizard Wheeze

'Although we've never met,' writes Roger G. Matson, a 'specialist computer programmer', 'I've taken the liberty of posting you a business proposition.' Rodge reckons he can potentially add $200,000 a year to my annual income. This *is* exciting as my only other possibilities are winning the potential lottery and potentially marrying James Packer.

Clearing out my post-office box, I noticed that others received the same unaddressed, four-page proposal. Rodge (although we've never met, I think I can take the liberty of calling him Rodge) told me that 'as a professional person, you are obviously intelligent and disciplined. I am also making the bold assumption that you like money and that you are reasonably ambitious!'

It's uncanny. Except for the disciplined bit. And I don't know about intelligent, because I've been going very stupid on an allergy-seeking de-toxing diet of vegetables, Brazil nuts and gravel. (Maybe I'm allergic to the gravel.) Also, I'm not that ambitious, really. And professional is a bit debatable. Apart from that, Rodge is on the button—although it's not actually money I like, it's the stuff you can do with it.

Rodge also writes that a person in my profession should have a lazy fifty thousand to invest in his proposal. Given that as far as Rodge knows I might be an unemployed freelance ferret fondler, this seems a bit of a stretch.

Rodge cleverly avoids being outed as a former bankrupt by saying so himself. He explains how he subsequently became a computer programmer and wrote a 'paper' about greyhound racing. 'I sensed,' says Rodge, 'a fine thread of predictability woven into the general lunacy of the race track.' He wrote a computer program for betting, and says it now earns him a million dollars a year, working ten hours a week. Now Rodge wants to share it. With us.

'Let me explain why,' writes Rodge. 'My wife has recently taken delivery of a new Mercedes sports coupe and I have just taken delivery of a nice little six-speed manual 911 Porsche to compliment [sic] my Rolls Royce and three Harley Davidsons. I've also now set an Australian record by contracting to purchase for $2.8 million a beachhouse at Noosa.' Rodge plans to buy holiday houses in France, Miami, Florida (not Miami, Tasmania) and Switzerland and set up a private school in Brisbane 'with an emphasis on good, old-fashioned values'.

Rodge wants to sell us his computer system idea and this 'investment in the...program will be only $45,000.00 plus a 10 per cent royalty on your profits for your first five years. Five thousand dollars must be also set aside as an investment bank.'

But first, Rodge wants us to know a few more things about his life:

'I live in a restored colonial mansion with crystal chandeliers and marble fireplaces. I have a 2.8 million–dollar, three-level beachhouse with glass elevator which is arguably the best beachhouse in the world. My children have attended the best private schools and we travel overseas as a family at least twice a year. My wife and I eat in the finest restaurants and every morning I work out for two hours with my personal health and fitness trainer. I have a wonderful circle of genuine, down-to-earth friends. Despite my abundant wealth I prefer the company of everyday people.'

What the wonderful circle of everyday people think of Rodge blathering on about Porsches with crystal private school trainer elevators is not recorded. I've decided that although Rodge's offer is very kind, if I had a lazy $50,000 I wouldn't be betting it on animals running around in a circle.

Somebody's just informed me that if I were married to James Packer I'd probably have to sleep with him. Good Lord. And furthermore, I'd probably have to meet him at some point. So much for THAT cunning plan.

# Getting Real

Have you gazed upon any real estate agents lately? Mostly they wear navy blue lounge-suits and disappear in a flash of industrial strength teeth, a miasma of men's cologne (formerly aftershave) and a late model Porsche/Merc/ BMW/Batmobile with vanity number plates saying things like SELL, BOOM, M.B.T.Y (Mine's Bigger Than Yours) and L.L.P.O.F (Liar, Liar, Pants on FIRE).

We plan to sell the house of my paramour Des Tiny's Aunty Ivy, who wants to move to the South of France and live out her last years with gin, Uncle Ern's super and middle-range gigolos. So the renovator's dream worker's cottage EXUDING potential and close to all amenities will be auctioned. Or, as Aunty Ivy says, or kitchenned.

We have been interviewing real estate agents who come to the door in twos, looking like well-lunched Mormons, not a member of the female persuasion to be seen. Some make up for this by speaking euphoniously to any women in the vicinity as if they were human beings likely to have an equal say in the selling of their own property.

Some prefer not to, instead gripping any available BLOKE in the vicinity most FIRMLY by the hand, looking him straight in the eye as if to say, 'What say we slip off to a Greek wrestling match to discuss market prices while the little ladies here do whatever they do when we're not around, which is a matter I've not devoted much time to considering. Whaddayer say, buddy? Let's ditch the skirts.'

Des pointed out that this inability to actually SEE women in the same room could be a problem if a woman wanted to buy Aunty Ivy's house. Because the attempted vendor would be saying things like, 'Hello. I want to buy this house', and the real estate agent would be saying, 'Where's your manly bidder?', 'What are you doing out alone?' and 'I can't hear a word you're saying madam, you don't have a penis.'

One couple of real estate agents came in and said, 'The place looks shocking. Who lives here?'

Aunty Ivy stepped up. 'I do, young man.'

'Get out, wrinkly. Vacant possession—always easier to sell.'

Another couple of besuited agents arrived. 'What do we need to do to make you…TAKE us?' they breathed, like Marilyn Monroe. Aunty Ivy had to be restrained. She thought the gigolo phase had been moved forward.

Many of the agents told us her house was worth about $567 million which isn't bad for a three-roomed fibro humpy in a swamp. Apparently they come round the night before the auction and tell you the market's in freefall and you might get $3.50.

Meanwhile, back at the residential turret which Des and me rent from another real estate agent, a debacle ensued, involving next-door's plumbing, our plumbing, the plumbing under the shed, all the plumbing imaginable and what can only be described as a babbling brook of raw sewage. On second thoughts, maybe it was us babbling, when we saw it. As we explained to one or two of the real estate agents, we know it when we see it.

# QUESTIONS

Would somebody have a word with Senator Pauline Harradine or whatever his name is and the other politicians who think that safe, early pregnancy termination should be impossible to obtain? Tell them that we girls don't sit around thinking, 'God, I'm bored. I think I'll just pop out and get a pint of milk and an abortion.'

How come a guy who has successfully reduced the funding of family planning clinics and is against contraception gets to say that abortions should remain illegal? How come old male politicians who will never be pregnant, who get paid really well—and whose secretaries have been known to remind them of their children's birthdays and send the present across a couple of state borders—get to make these decisions?

Also, did you see that guy on the TV? Is Senator Harradine about 9000 years old or what? It may work in the Tasmanian sheep industry, but could somebody tell him, and the prime minister, that compulsory breeding is out of fashion for humans?

I have some other questions:

• Why are all the clothes in the shops lime green and orange? Is there a dye shortage or did all the frock fondlers have some kind of mass citrus hallucination?

• How can the executive producer of the TV show 'Friends', Kevin Bright, tell *Who* magazine that the show 'is a little piece of your own life'? Have you ever met anyone as painstakingly groomed as any *one* cast member of 'Friends'? (Jennifer Aniston's hair alone must be holding down half the budget per episode.) Perhaps the show is a wee bit of Kev's life, as Kev is probably a shell-pink, muscly guy who drives a BMW Z3 around the joint, collecting his manicurist, his personal trouser arranger and his sideburn consultant and then going out for intravenous cafe latte.

• What have they done with Alexander Downer?

• What does Gareth Evans really need? In a recent interview he described the position of opposition as 'impotent' and shortly thereafter added that issues raised from opposition were not as 'sexy'. If sex is power and power is sex, why do we bother having two discrete words for 'em?

• Why doesn't the road smell nice when it rains in winter?

• What happened to Kimberley Davies's eyebrows? Has there been a ransom note?

• There are a couple of ferals in my neighbourhood who have purchased motorised scooters (the old scooters, like planks on wheels with the perpendicular long handlebars). They stand up on them and putter around at about 0.03 kilometres an hour with the engine sounding like indignant, electrified bees. My question is: Why don't they realise how pathetically nerdy they look and SHUT UP?

• Why don't state governments capitalise on the hospital crises by licensing casinos to take bets on how many people are screaming on trolleys in corridors at any given time and what are the odds of them surviving the night? Surely they could get some more money from the Medicare budget for marketing.

I have some answers too:

• When the aliens in *Independence Day* have whacked out the satellites, the USA bosses around the other world armies by morse code. The question is: If we get invaded by the Betentacled Ones on Monday, will we be ready? Why waste our time buying cruise missiles when we should be buying wee morse-code machiney thingies?

Wing Commander Ken Llewellyn, senior public affairs officer with the Australian Air Force and UFO spokes-hat says that although the air force doesn't teach morse code any more, our 800 or so pilots are still expected to be proficient in it, because it's used with some navigational aids. (In groovier air force circles the international morse code for SOS is now ordering three short blacks, three long blacks and then another three short blacks.)

Mr Llewellyn has written a book about 'paranormal experience in the military' called *Flight into the Ages* and he says due to reports of unexplained thingies, one 'can't dismiss easily' the existence of UFOs. Well, we hope we've scared him into brushing up on his morse code.

• How many angels can sit on the head of a pin? The Catholic Communications Office referred me to Monsignor Hart, a vicar-general who relayed the message: 'Angels are spiritual beings and as such don't occupy space.'

'It depends on how big the pin is and how adroit the angels might be,' says Father Mark Coleridge, the master of the Catholic Theological College of Melbourne, rather adroit himself. (Davo from my baseball team said, 'One very uncomfortable angel.') The National Council of Churches office in Sydney never rang back. Can't think why.

# MORE QUESTIONS

• Whose idea was it to suggest that blackcurrants have wobbly bits? In a TV ad for a blackcurrant drink, there's an animated cartoon of little blackcurrants with legs and arms and big blinky eyes running about a paddock—as blackcurrants are wont to do in the minds of some advertising types. This is disturbing enough, without the dawning horror that on the blackcurrants are tiny fig leaves strategically placed to hide mythical blackcurrant private parts.

The supposedly boy blackcurrant has one fig leaf and the allegedly girly blackcurrant has three, because of course you wouldn't want anybody impressionable getting a load of some berry's bosoms. Must impressionable children be subjected to this sort of twee, psychosexual fruit humbuggery?

• Why does society accept that of the doctors on duty at a major teaching hospital, several will have been on duty for the length of an average Test match? Or does this only happen on telly shows? If somebody had been on shift for eighteen hours you wouldn't even let them cut your hair, let alone decide your medical emergency treatment.

• What is the point of these stupid research projects we keep reading about, and who is funding them? Last week, newspapers reported that researchers at Leeds University in England had found that if you separate gerbils who have been lifelong mates, they will get depressed. Thanks for that. Isn't it time we left gerbils to their own devices and stopped sullying their reputations with unseemly rumours concerning Richard Gere or taking up their valuable time with this kind of stupid science?

• Has anyone else noticed that the ad campaign for the SBS series called 'Hitler's Henchmen' featured a naked baby with a Hitler moustache, and the ad campaign for the film *Children of the Revolution* features a naked baby with a Stalin moustache? What's next? Some poor tot tricked up in a Jeff Kennett wig or a Maggie Thatcher string of pearls?

• Isn't it fascinating that Lady Susan Renouf can lose more than $920,000 worth of jewellery and not ring the cops? In a statement to the rozzers, her ladyship said, 'I had been aware that most of this jewellery was missing but I didn't know what had happened to it and I was reluctant to say anything or accuse anybody.'

At the trial of her ladyship's former housekeeper, Lady Susan said that she thought she had 'misplaced' a matching bracelet, earrings and ring set made from emeralds, diamonds, rubies and sapphires worth $50,000, until she saw them hanging off another person who didn't know she was flashing around some hot rocks.

Other items which went inexplicably missing included a gold and diamond brooch, gold and diamond bracelet, diamond necklace, ruby and diamond bracelet, diamond pendants, diamond and sapphire earrings and ring, diamond earrings, gold pendant, gold and diamond earrings, diamond earrings, diamond and sapphire bangle, gemstone bracelet, gold ring, diamond bracelet, and a lifesize stuffed rhino studded with 140,000 giant rubies. Sorry, I made that last one up. That would be ostentatious and vulgar, wouldn't it?

• What sort of woman would spend money on 'CURVES' (trademark registered)? CURVES (trademark registered) are basically pink plasticcy thingies you stick into each cup of a bra. The reason for the thingies is that they sit under or around a real breast and make it look fatter. (For those of you who are interested, sadly, the CURVES [trademark registered] mob don't sell false botties.)

The manufacturers claim that the thingies 'feel just like breast tissue—soft and supple with a natural amount of firmness'. If this is the case I think the cup of a bra is the wrong place for them. To save women the palaver, men should carry them around in their trouser pockets. If women need something to put in a bra, why not try a hot-cross bun (over) or a banana (under)? These can be easily whipped out during moments of intimacy and popped aside for a reviving snack.

# A Fluff on All Their Houses

## Plague the First: Mrs Wispies

We are inundated with the type of woman so willowy she bends with the wind, with such drifting long hair she has to peep through it, and with such delicate sensibilities she has to whisper like the tiniest breath of dandelion fluff, even if she's ordering lunch ('A cup of chamomile tea if no chamomiles were killed in the process and half a fairy pikelet please') in tones as faint as a Volkswagen indicator light.

Mrs Wispy as a genre is best explained by the performance of Claire Danes in Mr Luhrmann's fine film of Romeo and Juliet. If ever there was a Mrs Wispy it was that Capulet girl, mooning around the house and languishing on every available ottoman.

Although one does wonder why Juliet doesn't say, instead of 'Wherefore art thou Romeo?', 'For Christ's sake, Romeo, go and get some dry togs on.' Juliet is the only person allowed to be Mrs Wispy as she has a perfectly good excuse—she is a fictional character. Anybody else still doing it needs to be told to stop putting on the dog.

## Plague the Second: Muscle-Weirdos

The latest edition of *Australian Ironman* magazine is padded out with photographs of men looking like deep-fried exploding willies. (I'm sorry but there's no other way to describe it, except 'a condom full of walnuts', and Clive James already did that.) Then there are the women muscle-weirdos.

This magazine is so obsessed with an obsession, and so used to the idea of people looking like self-constructing freaks, it doesn't even mention the fact that many of the women body builders look like nothing at all so much as muscle-bound, unconvincing drag queens. It's intriguing to study their photographs and try to work out what is the essence of woman they have lost, or is it an essence of male they have taken on?

It can't just be body shape, because people come in all shapes and sizes—although women don't ever come in these shapes and sizes without a lot of work and in some cases one suspects serious steroid use.

There is an elusive something in the line of the jaw perhaps, or the fact that the lipstick and tiny bikini tops on bookends that used to be breasts seem to be trying so hard to re-feminise what has become not so much masculine as unrecognisably inhuman.

The enormous, rippling muscles on arms, thighs, and shoulders make extreme body builders of both sexes look like another species entirely—neither man nor woman, but tragic, tortured narcissists desperate for prizes and approval. Relax, gang, it won't kill you.

PLAGUE THE THIRD: NOUVEAU BIMBOS
Grown women who talk in weeny ickle baby giggly tweeny voices and act as dumb as toast, but pretend they're 'strong women' because they make money doing it. If you thought this plague had been conquered by seventies feminism, think again—Goldie Hawn might have given it up for producing movies, but there's a whole new gang of

unbearably girly girls to rise up like the living dead.

'Well (tee-hee) hiya, guys. Does this next song of yours, you know, mean anything, or anything?' (nouveau bimbo radio announcer) or 'Goodness me, Minister/viewer/co-host, are those my enormously rambunctious bosoms making a run for it from the top of my heaving bodice?' (nouveau bimbo TV show host) and 'Darling, you're so good at complicated things' (nouveau bimbos everywhere).

In very severe cases, a nouveau bimbo will suck on her finger (think Juliette Lewis, rather than Capulet). This is the cue for anybody imbued with sisterhood to start slapping the nouveau bimbo for her own good.

PLAGUE THE FOURTH: MISPLACED STOICISM
Anyone who believes that playing tennis in 61-degree heat is acceptable is probably the sort of person who thinks a nice meal for athletes would be a boiled house brick and a cup of sump oil followed by a damned good thrashing with a fence paling.

A plague on all their houses.

# A ROSE BY ANY OTHER ROBBO

Early on in the history of humankind, back in the first wave of popularity for the leopard skin thigh-boot look, people had nicknames such as Og and Erg. These names were kept deliberately short for ease of communicating quickly, as in, 'Og! Look out for that giant diplodocus! No, the one behind the muttobuttosaurus near the Tyran-nosau…ooh. That's got to hurt.'

This convention was kept by the English, who had people called The Duke of Ponconfordshire on Whirrgate and the Honourable Peregrine Fortesque Bicycle-Chain Francine di Bordeaux the Fifth on his mother's side. This was more easily handled by saying, 'Pass the krugerrands, Binky, and splash a bit more port in Ponko's Waterford.'

Australians have since taken the tradition of nicknames to new heights. If the name can be shortened, it shall be. If the name cannot be shortened, it shall be lengthened— Mr Ng will become Ingie, and Rose becomes Rosie. Where else but Australia would whole banks be run by people called Nugget and Nobby?

If Boutros Boutros Ghali were Australian, he'd be nicknamed Booty. If he was a particularly jovial bloke he might have been promoted to Booto. Although this would have caused confusion on fact-finding missions to Pakistan. It is a measure of the Australian determination to give nicknames that somebody as staid as the news-reader Brian Henderson is called Hendo. And if you watch those sports programs, everyone's name ends in O:

254

Clelo, Rabbitohs, he's just kicked a goalo through the postos and now we'll take a short breako, matey.

McDonald's is Maccas and so is anybody with Scottish or Irish heritago. A girl from Japan called Tomoko is swiftly re-named Thommo. In the realm of the obvious, people with cute ears are called Wingnut and men who survived typical rugby incidents are called Leadnuts. Occasionally, there is irony. Tiny Tim was tall. People with red hair are called Blue.

We don't seem to do so well with politicians. I mean, can you see anybody calling Jeff Kennett 'Jeffo'? Peter Costello-oh? I don't think so. Bob Hawke was called the Silver Budgie and most of the nicknames for Paul Keating would get you an on-the-spot obscenity fine. But at least they had some. The best we can do for the prime minister is 'Little Johnny Howard', which lacks the impact of 'Pig Iron Bob', 'Black Jack' McEwen and 'Diamond Jim' McClelland.

Our singers and musicians have a long way to go, too. I mean, Barnsey, Farnsey and Merrill have nothing on Fats Waller, Muddy Waters, Duck Dunn, Iggy Pop, Smokey Robinson, Southside Johnny, Ringo Starr, Bubba Thrasher, Sly Stone, Johnny Rotten, Sid Vicious, Ice T, Sister Sledge, Me'shell, (Dweezil Zappa is disqualified for having a real name), Howlin' Wolf, Blind Snooks Eaglin', Blind Lemon Jefferson and Blind Willie Johnson. The closest we got was Little Patti, and she could see. (We did have a singer called William Shakespeare but he's disqualified for singing crap songs.)

This may be something of a flow-on from more

innovative lyrics. Russell Morris's 'Omm mow ma-mow' effort in 'The Real Thing', while similar to 'Papa oom mow mow' by The Rivingtons has nothing on lyrics like 'Doo-lang, doo-lang', 'Da doo ron ron', 'Be bop a lula', 'Doo wah diddy diddy', 'Woolly bully', 'Sh-boom, sh-boom', and 'Awopbopaloobopalopbamboom'. Not to mention the inspired 'Wang dang doodle'. And don't forget The Police's 'Duh doo doo doo, duh dah dah dah, that's all I want to say to you' a believable phrase from a man called Sting, joining the pantheon of people who make up their own one-shot nicknames to sound more cool.

Cher, Madonna, Blondie and Prince are in this bracket, although Prince turned out to be the type of Amanda who won't be called Mandy or a Richard who won't answer to Dick. He changed his nickname to a symbol and nobody has shouted him a beer since.

# GOODNIGHT SWEET FRUITCAKE

Sadly, this is my last column. Try this short quiz to find out the reason:

(a) Overwhelmed by jealousy, I got shickered at a News Ltd cocktail party and put chicken vol-au-vents in the editor's pumps while she was off executing a spirited hokey-pokey with the artiste formerly known as Julio Iglesias. Upon sobering up to a level of unparalleled mortification I moved to Majorca. Or:

(b) Alert readers may recall my recent whingeing about not having any of my own loinfruit to perform hilarious and cute acts to furnish me with material for my published musings. I explained the trouble I was having with my Tama-gotchi electronic toy baby which kept carking it. Shortly after, as a result of a night of passion—all right, two nights—with a dishy sailor—all right, two sailors—and the failure of modern contraception to get near 100 per cent in the tickety boo department, I found myself slightly up the duff.

Realising that I had to spare my readers the appalling prospect of hearing about every adorable poop of my naval offspring, I took the only honourable course possible and suggested that the editor replace the musings with the Warwick Farm racing results until the kid grew up, rebelled, joined the air force and left home in disgrace. Or:

(c) After reading yet another bloody newspaper story about what a decent bloke the deputy prime minister Tim Fischer is, and descending into a childish left-wing snit, I chained myself to the elevator in the offices of a firm of libel lawyers which I chose at random from the classified section of the *Sporting Globe*, with a sign reading 'Tim Fischer Is a Big Nancy Poo-Head Nerny Nerny Ner'. I was called to the office of the National Party executive, taken down the back paddock, and shot point-blank in the fetlock. Or:

(d) On my way to the corner shop the other day a divinely gorgeous man rode up on a white Shetland pony and exclaimed: 'Aren't you wearing Spice Girls Impulse eau du parfum, blue-eyes?'

'Why yes,' I replied.

'Well, you little green-eyed she-cat!' said the dark stranger with brooding eyebrows, quirking his manhood. 'I can tell by your flashing grey eyes and heaving bodice that the idea of being ravished by me is not unattractive.'

'Actually, that is my ferret Waldo,' I replied airily, 'who likes to hide in my singlet. And if there is any ravishing to be done I should like the first crack at it.' Me and the Prince (for it was he) (were him) (whatever) flew to the Bahamas where I am writing this on the balcony of the Princess Hotel. I shall get one of the minions to transfer it to a piece of paper and post it.

Alert readers who are leaning towards answer (b) are somewhat closer to the truth although may be lacking in romantic spirit, or a sailor. If you answered (a) you're on drugs. Those who picked (c) are developing dangerous paranoid tendencies, but I like you. And as for those who opted for (d) I thank you. As I thank all my lovely readers, except that weird guy from Queensland who keeps writing letters on the back of brown paper bags. He can get stuffed.

*Also from Kaz Cooke*

The Arts of Beauty and Hints to Gentlemen
on the Art of Fascinating
**Lola Montez**

Cartoons by **Kaz Cooke**

Lola Montez was the greatest show-off on earth. Born in
1818, she was famous for being rowdy, wicked and gorgeous.
She travelled to all corners of the earth, seducing royalty,
performing sexy dances and throwing tantrums. She drove
men mad with a glimpse of her breasts and horsewhipped
those who insulted her, including an Australian reporter.

In this smart and hilarious guide to beauty, Lola Montez
offers a bizarre series of hints on everything from make-up
to hair disasters. And she has a word or two of indispensable
advice for men who want to seduce women.

With her marvellous cartoons and introduction to Lola's life
Kaz Cooke has paid homage to the original Modern Girl.
If you've ever wondered whether squeezing orange juice
into your eyes will brighten them, or tried to charm a girl
by peering down her cleavage, *The Arts of Beauty* is the
book for you.

'This book is funny...full of ticklish observations on the
preoccupations of gender.' Kendall Hill, *Age*

'First published in 1858, the original text is now
accompanied by Kaz Cooke's hilarious cartoons, so that
all modern Nineties' women can benefit from Montez's
theories on beauty, described as a mixture of sensible savvy
and absolute nonsense.' *Elle*

216pp, hardback, rrp$19.95, ISBN 1 875847 39 1

Still the Two
**John Clarke**

*Mr Howard, thanks for joining us.*
Pleasure.

*It must just have been the biggest buzz. Did you ever think you'd win an Oscar?*
No I didn't, although it was a dream role.

*Why was it such a perfect role for you?*
Well I think it was the magic of the guy; little guy; typical of his time, confused, slightly peculiar.

*How is he confused?*
He's supposed to be a leader and he doesn't do any leading. He has a kind of psychological crisis. He can't decide what to do.

*Who is he supposed to be leading?*
At one stage he's got himself into the position where he's running an entire country.

*Oh dear. And he doesn't know what he's doing?*
Hasn't got a clue.

*So what does he do?*
Oh, you'll have to see the film.

'Laugh till you drop.'—*Examiner*

'Most of us are familiar with the John Clarke/Bryan Dawe political interviews from their broadcasts on radio and television, but they take on a whole new twist when they are read.'—*Sydney Morning Herald*

184pp, paperback, rrp$19.95, ISBN 1 875847 52 9